Allyn
and
Bacon

Research Navigator Guide

Education

Eugene F. Provenzo, Jr.
University of Miami

Linda R. Barr
University of the Virgin Islands

PEARSON

Boston | New York | San Francisco
Mexico City | Montreal | Toronto | London | Madrid | Munich | Paris
Hong Kong | Singapore | Tokyo | Cape Town | Sydney

For related titles and support materials, visit our online catalog at
www.ablongman.com

ISBN   0-205-40829-X

Printed in the United States of America

10 9 8 7 6 5 4 3 2 1   08 07 06 05 04 03

Contents

Research Navigator Guide: Education

Your professor assigns a research paper or group report that's due in two weeks—and you need to make sure you have up-to-date, credible information. Where do you begin? Today, the easiest answer is the Internet—because it can be so convenient and there is so much information out there. But therein lies part of the problem. How do you know if the information is reliable and from a trustworthy source?

Research Navigator Guide: Education is designed to help you select and evaluate research from the Web to help you find the best and most credible information you can. Throughout this guide, you'll find:

- **A Quick Guide to Research Navigator.** All you need to know to get started with Research Navigator™, a research database that gives you immediate access to hundreds of scholarly journals and other popular publications, such as *Scientific American, U.S. News & World Report,* and many others.
- **A practical and to-the-point discussion of search engines.** Find out which search engines are likely to get you the information you want and how to phrase your searches for the most effective results.
- **Detailed information on evaluating online sources.** Locate credible information on the Web and get tips for thinking critically about Web sites.
- **Citation guidelines for Web resources.** Learn the proper citation guidelines for Web sites, email messages, listservs, and more.
- **Web activities for Education.** Explore the various ways you can use the Web in your courses through these online exercises.
- **Web links for Education.** Begin your Web research with the discipline-specific sources listed in this section. Also included is information about Web resources offered by Allyn & Bacon—these sites are designed to give you an extra boost in your education courses.

So before running straight to your browser, take the time to read through this copy of *Research Navigator Guide: Education* and use it as a reference for all of your Web research needs.

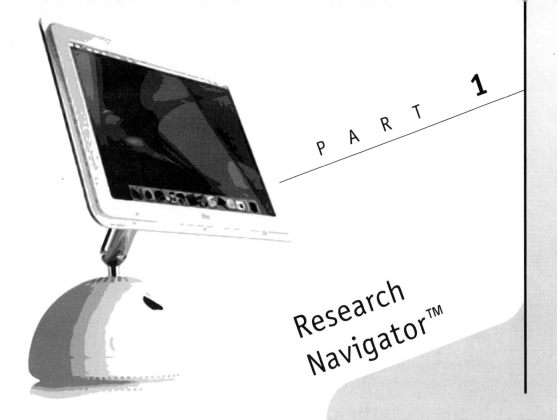

P A R T **1**

Research
Navigator™

What Is Research Navigator™?

Research Navigator™ is the easiest way for you to start a research assignment or paper.

Research Navigator™ includes three databases of dependable source material to get your research process started:

1. EBSCO's ContentSelect™ Academic Journal and Abstract Database, organized by subject, contains 50–100 of the leading academic journals per discipline. Instructors and students can search the online journals by keyword, topic, or multiple topics. Articles include abstract and citation information and can be cut, pasted, emailed, or saved for later use.

2. The *New York Times* Search by Subject Archive is organized by academic subject and searchable by keyword, or multiple keywords. Instructors and students can view full-text articles from the world's leading journalists from *The New York Times*. The *New York Times* Search by Subject Archive is available exclusively to instructors and students through Research Navigator™.

3. Link Library, organized by subject, offers editorially selected "Best of the Web" sites. Link libraries are continually scanned and kept up to date, providing the most relevant and accurate links for research assignments.

In addition, Research Navigator™ includes extensive online content detailing the steps in the research process including:

- Starting the Research Process
- Finding and Evaluating Sources
- Citing Sources
- Internet Research
- Using your Library
- Starting to Write

To begin using Research Navigator™, you must first register using the personal access code that appears in the front cover of this book. Follow the registration instructions on the inside front cover.

Getting Started

From the Research Navigator™ homepage, you have easy access to all of the site's main features, including a quick route to the three exclusive databases of source content that will be discussed in greater detail on the following pages. If you are new to the research process, you may want to start by clicking the *Research Process* tab, located in the upper right hand section of the page. Here you will find extensive help on all aspects of the research process, including:

- Introduction to the Research Paper
- Gathering Data

- Searching the Internet
- Evaluating Sources
- Organizing Ideas
- Writing Notes
- Drafting the Paper
- Academic Citation Styles (MLA, APA, CME, and more)
- Blending Reference Material into Your Writing
- Practicing Academic Integrity
- Revising
- Proofreading
- Editing the Final Draft

For those of you who are already familiar with the research process, you already know that the first step in completing a research assignment or research paper is to select a topic. (In some cases, your instructor may assign you a topic.) According to James D. Lester in *Writing Research Papers,* choosing a topic for the research paper can be easy (any topic will serve) yet very complicated (an informed choice is critical). He suggests selecting a person, a person's work, or a specific issue to study—President George W. Bush, John Steinbeck's *Of Mice and Men,* or learned dexterity with Nintendo games. Try to select a topic that will meet three demands.

1. It must examine a significant issue.
2. It must address a knowledgeable reader and carry that reader to another level of knowledge.
3. It must have a serious purpose, one that demands analysis of the issues, argues from a position, and explains complex details.

You can find more tips from Lester in the *Research Process* section of Research Navigator™.

Research Navigator Guide: Education

EBSCO's ContentSelect Academic Journal and Abstract Database

EBSCO's ContentSelect Academic Journal and Abstract Database contains scholarly, peer-reviewed journals (such as the *Journal of Clinical Psychology*). A scholarly journal is an edited collection of articles written by various authors and is published several times per year. All the issues published in one calendar year comprise a volume of that journal. For example, the *American Sociological Review* published volume 65 in the year 2000. This journal is published six times a year, so issues 1–6 in volume 65 are the individual issues for that year. Each issue contains between 4 and 8 articles. Additionally, issues may contain letters from the editor, book reviews, and comments from authors. Each issue does not necessarily revolve around a common theme; most issues contain articles on many different topics.

Although similar to magazines in that they are published several times per year and contain articles on different topics, scholarly journals are NOT magazines. What sets them apart from popular magazines is that the content of each issue is peer-reviewed. The editor relies on these peer reviewers both to evaluate the articles and to decide if they should be accepted for publication. Academic journal articles adhere to strict scientific guidelines for methodology and theoretical grounding. The information in these articles is more scientific than information in a popular magazine, newspaper article, or on a Web page.

Using ContentSelect.   Here are some instructions and search tips to help you find articles for your research paper.

Step 1: **Select an academic subject and topic area.** When you first enter the database, you will see a list of disciplines. To search within a single academic subject, click the name of that subject. To search in more than one subject, hold down the alt or command key. In the space below where all the subjects are listed, enter a topic area. For example if you choose Psychology as a subject you might enter "Freud" as a topic area.

Step 2: **Basic Search.** Click the **GO** button to start your search. You will be brought to the *Basic Search* tab. Basic Search lets you search for articles using a variety of methods. You can select from: Standard Search, All Words, Any Words, or Exact Phrase. For more information on these options, click the **Search Tips** link at any time! After you have selected your method click **Search.**

Some ways to improve your search:

Tip 1: **AND, OR, and NOT.** In Standard Search, you can use AND, OR and NOT to create a broad or narrow search:

- **AND** searches for articles containing all of the words. For example, typing **education AND technology** will search for articles that contain **both** education AND technology.
- **OR** searches for articles that contains at least one of the terms. For example, searching for **education OR technology** will find articles that contain either education OR technology.
- **NOT** excludes words so that the articles will not include the word that follows "NOT." For example, searching for **education NOT technology** will find articles that contain the term education but NOT the term technology.

Tip 2: **Using All Words.** When you select the "All Words" option, you do not need to use the word AND—you will automatically search for articles that only contain all of the words. The order of the search words entered in does not matter. For example, typing **education technology** will search for articles that contain **both** education AND technology.

Tip 3: **Using Any Words.** After selecting the "Any Words" option, type words, a phrase, or a sentence in the window. ContentSelect will search for articles that contain any of the terms you typed (but will not search for words such as **in** and **the**). For example, type **rising medical costs in the United States** to find articles that contain *rising, medical, costs, United,* or *States.* To limit your search to find articles that contain exact terms, use *quotation marks*—for example, typing "United States" will only search for articles containing "United States."

Tip 4: **Using Exact Phrase.** Select this option to find articles containing an exact phrase. ContentSelect will search for articles that include all the words you entered, exactly as you entered them. For example, type **rising medical costs in the United States** to find articles that contain the exact phrase "rising medical costs in the United States."

Search by Article Number.

Each and every article in EBSCO's ContentSelect Academic Journal and Abstract Database is assigned its own unique article number. In some instances, you may know the exact article number for the journal article you want to retrieve. Perhaps you noted it during a prior research session on Research Navigator™. Such article numbers might also be found on the companion web site for your text, or in the text itself.

To retrieve a specific article, simply type that article number in the "Search by Article Number" field and click the **GO** button.

Advanced Search.

These tips will help you with an Advanced Search.

Step 1: To switch to an **Advanced Search**, from the Basic Search click the *AdvancedSearch* tab on the navigation bar, just under the EBSCO Host logo. The *AdvancedSearch* tab helps you focus your search using keyword searching, search history and limiters.

Step 2: Type the words you want to search for in the **Find** field.

Step 3: Click on **Field Codes** to see a list of available field codes for limiting your search. For example: AU-Author, will limit your search to an author. Enter one of these two-letter field codes before your search term. For example, if you enter AU-Smith, this will limit your results to SMITH in the Author field. For more information on field codes, click **Search Tips**. After you have added the appropriate Field Code to your topic, click **Search.**

Some ways to improve your search:

Tip 1: You can enter additional search terms in the **Find** field, and remember to use *and, or,* and *not* to connect multiple search terms (see Tip 1 under Basic Search for information on *and, or,* and *not*).

Tip 2: With Advanced Searches you can also use **Limiters** and **Expanders** to refine your search. For more information on Limiters and Expanders, click **Search Tips**.

The *New York Times* Search by Subject Archive

Newspapers, also known as periodicals because they are issued in periodic installments (e.g. daily, weekly, or monthly), provide contemporary information. Information in periodicals—journals, magazines, and newspapers—may be useful, or even critical, when you are ready to focus in on specific aspects of your topic, or to find more up-to-date information.

There are some significant differences between newspaper articles and journal articles, and you should consider the level of scholarship that is most appropriate for your research. Popular or controversial topics may not be well covered in journals, even though coverage in newspapers and "general interest" magazines like *Newsweek* and *Science* for that same topic may be extensive.

Research Navigator™ gives you access to a one-year, "search by subject" archive of articles from *The New York Times*. To learn more about *The New York Times,* visit **http://www.nytimes.com**.

Using the search-by-subject archive is easy. Simply type a word, or multiple words separated by commas, into the search box and click "go." You will see a list of articles that have appeared in the *New York Times* over the last year, sorted by most recent article first. You can further refine your search as needed. Articles can be printed or saved for later use in your research assignment. Be sure to review the citation rules for how to cite a newspaper article in endnotes or a bibliography.

"Best of the Web" Link Library

The third database included on Research Navigator™, Link Library, is a collection of Web links, organized by academic subject and key terms. To use this database, simply select an academic subject from the dropdown list, and then find the key term for the topic you are searching. Click on the key term and see a list of five to seven editorially reviewed Web sites that offer educationally relevant and reliable content. For example, if your research topic is "Allergies," you may want to select the academic subject Biology and then click on "Allergies" for links to web sites that explore this topic. Simply click on the alphabet bar to view other key terms in Biology, and their corresponding links. The web links in Link Library are monitored and updated each week, reducing your incidence of finding "dead" links.

Using Your Library

After you have selected your topic and gathered source material from the three databases of content on Research Navigator™, you may need to complete your research by going to your school library. Research Navigator™ does not try to replace the library, but rather helps you understand how to use library resources effectively and efficiently.

You may put off going to the library to complete research assignments or research papers because the library can seem overwhelming. Research Navigator™ provides a bridge to the library by taking you through a simple step-by-step overview of how to make the most of your library time. Written by a library scientist, the *Using Your Library* tab explains:

- Major types of libraries
- What the library has to offer
- How to choose the right library tools for a project
- The research process
- How to make the most of research time in the library

In addition, when you are ready to use the library to complete a research assignment or research paper, Research Navigator™ includes 31 discipline-specific "library guides" for you to use as a roadmap. Each guide includes an overview of the discipline's major subject databases, online journals, and key associations and newsgroups.

For more information and detailed walk-throughs, please visit
www.ablongman.com/aboutRN

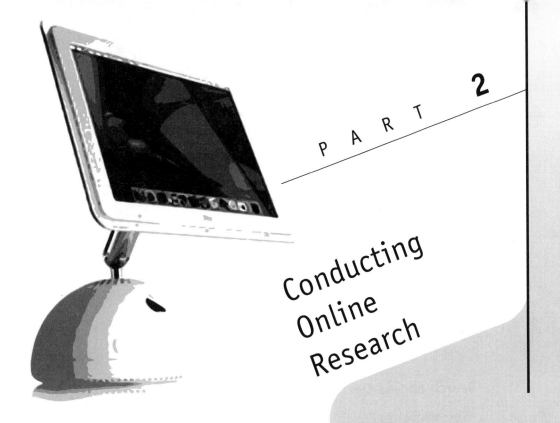

P A R T **2**

Conducting Online Research

Finding Sources:
Search Engines and Subject Directories

Your professor has just given you an assignment to give a five minute speech on the topic "gun control." After a (hopefully brief) panic attack, you begin to think of what type of information you need before you can write the speech. To provide an interesting introduction, you decide to involve your class by taking a straw poll of their views for and against gun control, and to follow this up by giving some statistics on how many Americans favor (and oppose) gun control legislation and then by outlining the arguments on both sides of the issue. If you already know the correct URL for an authoritative Web site like Gallup Opinion Polls (www.gallup.com) or other sites you are in great shape! However, what do you do when you don't have a clue as to which Web site would have information on your topic? In these cases, many, many people routinely (and mistakenly) go to Yahoo! and type in a single term (e.g., guns). This approach is sure to bring first a smile to your face when the results offer you 200,874 hits on your topic, but just as quickly make you grind your teeth in frustration when you start scrolling down the hit list and find sites that range from gun dealerships, to reviews of the video "Young Guns," to aging fan sites for "Guns and Roses."

Finding information on a specific topic on the Web is a challenge. The more intricate your research need, the more difficult it is to find the one or two Web sites among the billions that feature the information you want. This section is designed to help you to avoid frustration and to focus in on the right site for your research by using search engines, subject directories, and meta-sites.

Search Engines

Search engines (sometimes called search services) are becoming more numerous on the Web. Originally, they were designed to help users search the Web by topic. More recently, search engines have added features which enhance their usefulness, such as searching a particular part of the Web (e.g., only sites of educational institutions—dot.edu), retrieving just one site which the search engine touts as most relevant (like Ask Jeeves {www.aj.com}), or retrieving up to 10 sites which the search engine rank as most relevant (like Google {www.google.com}).

Search Engine Defined

According to Cohen (1999):

> "A search engine service provides a searchable database of Internet files collected by a computer program called a wanderer, crawler, robot, worm, or spider. Indexing is created from the collected files, and the results are presented in a schematic order. There are no selection criteria for the collection of files.
>
> A search service therefore consists of three components: (1) a spider, a program that traverses the Web from link to link, identifying and reading pages; (2) an index, a database containing a copy of each Web page gathered by the spider; and (3) a search engine mechanism, software that enables users to query the index and then returns results in a schematic order (p. 31)."

One problem students often have in their use of search engines is that they are deceptively easy to use. Like our example "guns," no matter what is typed into the handy box at the top, links to numerous Web sites appear instantaneously, lulling students into a false sense of security. Since so much was retrieved, surely SOME of it must be useful. WRONG! Many Web sites retrieved will be very light on substantive content, which is not what you need for most academic endeavors. Finding just the right Web site has been likened to finding diamonds in the desert.

As you can see by the definition above, one reason for this is that most search engines use indexes developed by machines. Therefore they are indexing terms not concepts. The search engine cannot tell the difference between the keyword "crack" to mean a split in the sidewalk and "crack" referring to crack cocaine. To use search engines properly takes some skill, and this chapter will provide tips to help you use search engines more effectively. First, however, let's look at the different types of search engines with examples:

TYPES OF SEARCH ENGINES		
TYPE	**DESCRIPTION**	**EXAMPLES**
1st Generation	• Non-evaluative, do not evaluate results in terms of content or authority. • Return results ranked by relevancy alone (number of times the term(s) entered appear, usually on the first paragraph or page of the site)	AltaVista (www.altavista.com/) Excite (www.excite.com) HotBot (www.HotBot.com) Infoseek (guide.infoseek.com) Ixquick Metasearch (ixquick.com) Lycos (www.lycos.com)
2nd Generation	• More creative in displaying results. • Results are ordered by characteristics such as: concept, document type, Web site, popularity, etc. rather than relevancy.	Ask Jeeves (www.aj.com/) Direct Hit (www.directhit.com/) Google! (www.google.com/) HotLinks (www.hotlinks.com/) Simplifind (www.simpli.com/) SurfWax (www.surfwax.com/) Also see Meta-Search engines below. EVALUATIVE SEARCH ENGINES About.Com (www.about.com) WebCrawler (www.webcrawler.com)
Commercial Portals	• Provide additional features such as: customized news, stock quotations, weather reports, shopping, etc. • They want to be used as a "one stop" Web guide. • They profit from prominent advertisements and fees charged to featured sites.	GONetwork (www.go.com/) Google Web Directory (directory.google.com/) LookSmart (www.looksmart.com/) My Starting Point (www.stpt.com/) Open Directory Project (dmoz.org/) NetNow (www.inetnow.com) Yahoo! (www.yahoo.com/)
Meta-Search Engines	Run searches on multiple search engines.	There are different types of meta-search engines. See the next 2 boxes.

(continued)

TYPES OF SEARCH ENGINES, *continued*		
TYPE	DESCRIPTION	EXAMPLES
Meta-Search Engines *Integrated Result*	• Display results for search engines in one list. • Duplicates are removed. • Only portions of results from each engine are returned.	Beaucoup.com (www.beaucoup.com/) Highway 61 (www.highway61.com) Cyber411(www.cyber411. com/) Mamma (www.mamma.com/) MetaCrawler (www. metacrawler.com/) Visisimo (www.vivisimo.com) Northern Light (www.nlsearch.com/) SurfWax (www.surfwax.com)
Meta-Search Engines *Non-Integrated Results*	• Comprehensive search. • Displays results from each search engine in separate results sets. • Duplicates remain. • You must sift through all the sites.	Dogpile (www.dogpile.com) Global Federated Search (jin.dis.vt.edu/fedsearch/) GoHip (www.gohip.com) Searchalot (www.searchalot.com) 1Blink (www.1blink.com) ProFusion (www. profusion.com/)

QUICK TIPS FOR MORE EFFECTIVE USE OF SEARCH ENGINES

1. Use a search engine:
   - When you have a narrow idea to search.
   - When you want to search the full text of countless Web pages
   - When you want to retrieve a large number of sites
   - When the features of the search engine (like searching particular parts of the Web) help with your search

2. Always use Boolean Operators to combine terms. Searching on a single term is a sure way to retrieve a very large number of Web pages, few, if any, of which are on target.
   - Always check search engine's HELP feature to see what symbols are used for the operators as these vary (e.g., some engines use the & or + symbol for AND).
   - Boolean Operators include:
     AND to narrow search and to make sure that **both** terms are included
       e.g:, children AND violence
     OR to broaden search and to make sure that **either** term is included
       e.g., child OR children OR juveniles
     NOT to **exclude** one term
       e.g., eclipse NOT lunar

Research Navigator Guide: Education

3. Use appropriate symbols to indicate important terms and to indicate phrases (Best Bet for Constructing a Search According to Cohen (1999): Use a plus sign (+) in front of terms you want to retrieve: +solar +eclipse. Place a phrase in double quotation marks: "solar eclipse" Put together: "+solar eclipse" "+South America").

4. Use word stemming (a.k.a. truncation) to find all variations of a word (check search engine HELP for symbols).
   - If you want to retrieve child, child's, or children use child* (some engines use other symbols such as !, #, or $)
   - Some engines automatically search singular and plural terms, check HELP to see if yours does.

5. Since search engines only search a portion of the Web, use several search engines or a meta-search engine to extend your reach.

6. Remember search engines are generally mindless drones that do not evaluate. Do not rely on them to find the best Web sites on your topic, use *subject directories* or meta-sites to enhance value (see below).

Finding Those Diamonds in the Desert: Using Subject Directories and Meta-sites

Although some search engines, like WebCrawler (www.webcrawler.com) do evaluate the Web sites they index, most search engines do not make any judgment on the worth of the content. They just return a long—sometimes very long—list of sites that contained your keyword. However, *subject directories* exist that are developed by human indexers, usually librarians or subject experts, and are defined by Cohen (1999) as follows:

> "A subject directory is a service that offers a collection of links to Internet resources submitted by site creators or evaluators and organized into subject categories. Directory services use selection criteria for choosing links to include, though the selectivity varies among services (p. 27)."

World Wide Web Subject directories are useful when you want to see sites on your topic that have been reviewed, evaluated, and selected for their authority, accuracy, and value. They can be real time savers for students, since subject directories weed out the commercial, lightweight, or biased Web sites.

Metasites are similar to subject directories, but are more specific in nature, usually dealing with one scholarly field or discipline. Some examples of subject directories and meta-sites are found in the table on the next page.

Choose subject directories to ensure that you are searching the highest quality Web pages. As an added bonus, subject directories periodically check Web links to make sure that there are fewer dead ends and out-dated links.

Research Navigator Guide: Education

Research Navigator Guide: Education

SMART SEARCHING—SUBJECT DIRECTORIES AND META-SITES	
TYPES—SUBJECT DIRECTORIES	EXAMPLES
General, covers many topics	Access to Internet and Subject Resources (www2.lib.udel.edu/subj/)
	Best Information on the Net (BIOTN) (http://library.sau.edu/bestinfo/)
	Federal Web Locator (www.infoctr.edu/fwl/)
	Galaxy (galaxy.einet.net)
	INFOMINE: Scholarly Internet Resource Collections (infomine.ucr.edu/)
	InfoSurf: Resources by Subject (www.library.ucsb.edu/subj/)
	Librarian's Index to the Internet (www.lii.org/)
	Martindale's "The Reference Desk" (www-sci.lib.uci.edu/ HSG/ref.html)
	PINAKES: A Subject Launchpad (www.hw.ac.uk/libWWW/irn/pinakes/pinakes.html)
	Refdesk.com (www.refdesk.com)
	Search Engines and Subject Directories (College of New Jersey) (www.tcnj.edu/~library/research/internet_ search.html)
	Scout Report Archives (www.scout.cs.wisc.edu/archives)
	Selected Reference Sites (www.mnsfld.edu/depts/lib/ mu~ref.html)
	WWW Virtual Library (http://vlib.org)
Subject Oriented	
• Communication Studies	The Media and Communication Studies Site (www.aber.ac.uk/media)
	University of Iowa Department of Communication Studies (www.uiowa.edu/~commstud/resources)
• Cultural Studies	Sara Zupko's Cultural Studies Center (www.popcultures.com)
• Education	Educational Virtual Library (www.csu.edu.au/education/ library.html)
	ERIC [Education ResourcesInformation Center] (ericir.sunsite.syr.edu/)
	Kathy Schrock's Guide for Educators (kathyschrock.net/abceval/index.htm)
• Journalism	Journalism Resources (bailiwick.lib.uiowa.edu/journalism/)
	Journalism and Media Criticism page (www.chss.montclair.edu/english/furr/media.html)
• Literature	Norton Web Source to American Literature (www.wwnorton.com/naal)
	Project Gutenberg [Over 3,000 full text titles] (www.gutenberg.net)

SMART SEARCHING, *continued*	
TYPES—SUBJECT DIRECTORIES	EXAMPLES
• Medicine & Health	PubMed [National Library of Medicine's index to Medical journals, 1966 to present] (www.ncbi.nlm.nih.gov/PubMed/) RxList: The Internet Drug Index (rxlist.com) Go Ask Alice (www.goaskalice.columbia.edu) [Health and sexuality]
• Technology	CNET.com (www.cnet.com)

Another closely related group of sites are the *Virtual Library sites,* also referred to as Digital Library sites. Hopefully, your campus library has an outstanding Web site for both on-campus and off-campus access to resources. If not, there are several virtual library sites that you can use, although you should realize that some of the resources would be subscription based, and not accessible unless you are a student of that particular university or college. These are useful because, like the subject directories and meta-sites, experts have organized Web sites by topic and selected only those of highest quality.

You now know how to search for information and use search engines more effectively. In the next section, you will learn more tips for evaluating the information that you found.

VIRTUAL LIBRARY SITES	
PUBLIC LIBRARIES	
• Internet Public Library	www.ipl.org
• Library of Congress	lcweb.loc.gov/homepage/lchp.html
• New York Public Library	www.nypl.org
University/College Libraries	
• Bucknell	jade.bucknell.edu/
• Case Western	www.cwru.edu/uclibraries.html
• Dartmouth	www.dartmouth.edu/~library
• Duke	www.lib.duke.edu/
• Franklin & Marshall	www.library.fandm.edu
• Harvard	www.harvard.edu/museums/
• Penn State	www.libraries.psu.edu
• Princeton	infoshare1.princeton.edu
• Stanford	www.slac.stanford.edu/FIND/spires.html
• ULCA	www.library.ucla.edu

(continued)

Research Navigator Guide: Education

VIRTUAL LIBRARY SITES, *continued*

PUBLIC LIBRARIES

Other
• Perseus Project [subject specific—classics, supported by   www.perseus.tufts.edu
  grants from corporations and educational institutions]

BIBLIOGRAPHY FOR FURTHER READING

Books

Basch, Reva. (1996). Secrets of the Super Net Searchers.

Berkman, Robert I. (2000). *Find It Fast: How to Uncover Expert Information on Any Subject Online or in Print.* NY: HarperResource.

Glossbrenner, Alfred & Glossbrenner, Emily. (1999). *Search Engines for the World Wide Web,* 2nd Ed. Berkeley, CA: Peachpit Press.

Hock, Randolph, & Berinstein, Paula.. (1999). *The Extreme Searcher's Guide to Web Search Engines: A Handbook for the Serious Searcher.* Information Today, Inc.

Miller, Michael. *Complete Idiot's Guide to Yahoo!* (2000). Indianapolis, IN: Que.

Miller, Michael. *Complete Idiot's Guide to Online Search Secrets.* (2000). Indianapolis, IN: Que.

Paul, Nora, Williams, Margot, & Hane, Paula. (1999). *Great Scouts!: CyberGuides for Subject Searching on the Web.* Information Today, Inc.

Radford, Marie, Barnes, Susan, & Barr, Linda (2001). *Web Research: Selecting, Evaluating, and Citing* Boston. Allyn and Bacon.

Journal Articles

Cohen, Laura B. (1999, August). The Web as a research tool: Teaching strategies for instructors. *CHOICE Supplement* 3, 20–44.

Cohen, Laura B. (August 2000). Searching the Web: The Human Element Emerges. *CHOICE Supplement 37,* 17–31.

Introna, Lucas D., & Nissenbaum, Helen. (2000). Shaping the web: Why the politics of search engines matters. The Information Society, Vol. 16, No. 3, pp. 169–185.

Evaluating Sources on the Web

Congratulations! You've found a great Web site. Now what? The Web site you found seems like the perfect Web site for your research. But, are you sure? Why is it perfect? What criteria are you using to determine whether this Web site suits your purpose?

Think about it. Where else on earth can anyone "publish" information regardless of the *accuracy, currency,* or *reliability* of the information? The

Internet has opened up a world of opportunity for posting and distributing information and ideas to virtually everyone, even those who might post misinformation for fun, or those with ulterior motives for promoting their point of view. Armed with the information provided in this guide, you can dig through the vast amount of useless information and misinformation on the World Wide Web to uncover the valuable information. Because practically anyone can post and distribute their ideas on the Web, you need to develop a new set of *critical thinking skills* that focus on the evaluation of the quality of information, rather than be influenced and manipulated by slick graphics and flashy moving java script.

Before the existence of online sources, the validity and accuracy of a source was more easily determined. For example, in order for a book to get to the publishing stage, it must go through many critiques, validation of facts, reviews, editorial changes and the like. Ownership of the information in the book is clear because the author's name is attached to it. The publisher's reputation is on the line too. If the book turns out to have incorrect information, reputations and money can be lost. In addition, books available in a university library are further reviewed by professional librarians and selected for library purchase because of their accuracy and value to students. Journal articles downloaded or printed from online subscription services, such as Infotrac, ProQuest, EbscoHost, or other fulltext databases, are put through the same scrutiny as the paper versions of the journals.

On the World Wide Web, however, Internet service providers (ISPs) simply give Web site authors a place to store information. The Web site author can post information that may not be validated or tested for accuracy. One mistake students typically make is to assume that all information on the Web is of equal value. Also, in the rush to get assignments in on time, students may not take the extra time to make sure that the information they are citing is accurate. It is easy just to cut and paste without really thinking about the content in a critical way. However, to make sure you are gathering accurate information and to get the best grade on your assignments, it is vital that you develop your critical ability to sift through the dirt to find the diamonds.

Web Evaluation Criteria

So, here you are, at this potentially great site. Let's go though some ways you can determine if this site is one you can cite with confidence in your research. Keep in mind, ease of use of a Web site is an issue, but more important is learning how to determine the validity of data, facts, and statements for your use. The five traditional ways to verify a paper source can also be applied to your Web source: *accuracy, authority, objectivity, coverage,* and *currency.*

Evaluating Web Sites Using
Five Criteria to Judge Web Site Content

Accuracy—How reliable is the information?

Authority—Who is the author and what are his or her credentials?

Objectivity—Does the Web site present a balanced or biased point of view?

Coverage—Is the information comprehensive enough for your needs?

Currency—Is the Web site up to date?

Use additional criteria to judge Web site content, including

- **Publisher, documentation, relevance, scope, audience, appropriateness of format**, and **navigation**
- Judging whether the site is made up of **primary (original) or secondary (interpretive) sources**
- Determining whether the information is **relevant** to your research

Content Evaluation

Accuracy.   Internet searches are not the same as searches of library databases because much of the information on the Web has not been edited, whereas information in databases has. It is your responsibility to make sure that the information you use in a school project is accurate. When you examine the content on a Web site or Web page, you can ask yourself a number of questions to determine whether the information is accurate.

1. Is the information reliable?
2. Do the facts from your other research contradict the facts you find on this Web page?
3. Do any misspellings and/or grammar mistakes indicate a hastily put together Web site that has not been checked for accuracy?
4. Is the content on the page verifiable through some other source? Can you find similar facts elsewhere (journals, books, or other online sources) to support the facts you see on this Web page?
5. Do you find links to other Web sites on a similar topic? If so, check those links to ascertain whether they back up the information you see on the Web page you are interested in using.
6. Is a bibliography of additional sources for research provided? Lack of a bibliography doesn't mean the page isn't accurate, but having one allows you further investigation points to check the information.
7. Does the site of a research document or study explain how the data was collected and the type of research method used to interpret the data?

If you've found a site with information that seems too good to be true, it may be. You need to verify information that you read on the Web by cross-checking against other sources.

Authority.   An important question to ask when you are evaluating a Web site is, "Who is the author of the information?" Do you know whether the author is a recognized authority in his or her field? Biographical information, references to publications, degrees, qualifications, and organizational affiliations can help to indicate an author's authority. For example, if you are researching the topic of laser surgery citing a medical doctor would be better than citing a college student who has had laser surgery.

The organization sponsoring the site can also provide clues about whether the information is fact or opinion. Examine how the information was gathered and the research method used to prepare the study or report. Other questions to ask include:

1. Who is responsible for the content of the page? Although a webmaster's name is often listed, this person is not necessarily responsible for the content.
2. Is the author recognized in the subject area? Does this person cite any other publications he or she has authored?
3. Does the author list his or her background or credentials (e.g., Ph.D. degree, title such as professor, or other honorary or social distinction)?
4. Is there a way to contact the author? Does the author provide a phone number or email address?
5. If the page is mounted by an organization, is it a known, reputable one?
6. How long has the organization been in existence?
7. Does the URL for the Web page end in the extension .edu or .org? Such extensions indicate authority compared to dotcoms (.com), which are commercial enterprises. (For example, www.cancer.com takes you to an online drugstore that has a cancer information page; www.cancer.org is the American Cancer Society Web site.)

A good idea is to ask yourself whether the author or organization presenting the information on the Web is an authority on the subject. If the answer is no, this may not be a good source of information.

Objectivity.   Every author has a point of view, and some views are more controversial than others. Journalists try to be objective by providing both sides of a story. Academics attempt to persuade readers by presenting a logical argument, which cites other scholars' work. You need to look for two sided arguments in news and information sites. For academic papers, you need to determine how the paper fits within its discipline and whether the author is using controversial methods for reporting a conclusion.

Authoritative authors situate their work within a larger discipline. This background helps readers evaluate the author's knowledge on a particular

Research Navigator Guide: Education

subject. You should ascertain whether the author's approach is controversial and whether he or she acknowledges this. More important, is the information being presented as fact or opinion? Authors who argue for their position provide readers with other sources that support their arguments. If no sources are cited, the material may be an opinion piece rather than an objective presentation of information. The following questions can help you determine objectivity:

1. Is the purpose of the site clearly stated, either by the author or the organization authoring the site?
2. Does the site give a balanced viewpoint or present only one side?
3. Is the information directed toward a specific group of viewers?
4. Does the site contain advertising?
5. Does the copyright belong to a person or an organization?
6. Do you see anything to indicate who is funding the site?

Everyone has a point of view. This is important to remember when you are using Web resources. A question to keep asking yourself is, What is the bias or point of *view* being expressed here?

Coverage. Coverage deals with the breadth and depth of information presented on a Web site. Stated another way, it is about how much information is presented and how detailed the information is. Looking at the site map or index can give you an idea about how much information is contained on a site. This isn't necessarily bad. Coverage is a criteria that is tied closely to *your* research requirement. For one assignment, a given Web site may be too general for your needs. For another assignment, that same site might be perfect. Some sites contain very little actual information because pages are filled with links to other sites. Coverage also relates to objectivity You should ask the following questions about coverage:

1. Does the author present both sides of the story or is a piece of the story missing?
2. Is the information comprehensive enough for your needs?
3. Does the site cover too much, too generally?
4. Do you need more specific information than the site can provide?
5. Does the site have an objective approach?

In addition to examining what is covered on a Web site, equally revealing is what is not covered. Missing information can reveal a bias in the material. Keep in mind that you are evaluating the information on a Web site for your research requirements.

Currency. Currency questions deal with the timeliness of information. However, currency is more important for some topics than for others. For example, currency is essential when you are looking for technology related topics and current events. In contrast, currency may not be relevant when you are doing research on Plato or Ancient Greece. In terms of Web sites, currency also pertains to whether the site is being kept up to date and links are being maintained. Sites on the Web are sometimes abandoned by their owners. When people move or change jobs, they may neglect to remove theft site from the company or university server. To test currency ask the following questions:

1. Does the site indicate when the content was created?
2. Does the site contain a last revised date? How old is the date? (In the early part of 2001, a university updated their Web site with a "last up-dated" date of 1901! This obviously was a Y2K problem, but it does point out the need to be observant of such things!)
3. Does the author state how often he or she revises the information? Some sites are on a monthly update cycle (e.g., a government statistics page).
4. Can you tell specifically what content was revised?
5. Is the information still useful for your topic? Even if the last update is old, the site might still be worthy of use *if* the content is still valid for your research.

Relevancy to Your Research: Primary versus Secondary Sources

Some research assignments require the use of primary (original) sources. Materials such as raw data, diaries, letters, manuscripts, and original accounts of events can be considered primary material. In most cases, these historical documents are no longer copyrighted. The Web is a great source for this type of resource.

Information that has been analyzed and previously interpreted is considered a secondary source. Sometimes secondary sources are more appropriate than primary sources. If, for example, you are asked to analyze a topic or to find an analysis of a topic, a secondary source of an analysis would be most appropriate. Ask yourself the following questions to determine whether the Web site is relevant to your research:

1. Is it a primary or secondary source?
2. Do you need a primary source?
3. Does the assignment require you to cite different types of sources? For example, are you supposed to use at least one book, one journal article, and one Web page?

You need to think critically, both visually and verbally, when evaluating Web sites. Because Web sites are designed as multimedia hypertexts, nonlinear texts, visual elements, and navigational tools are added to the evaluation process.

Help in Evaluating Web Sites.   One shortcut to finding high-quality Web sites is using subject directories and meta-sites, which select the Web sites they index by similar evaluation criteria to those just described. If you want to learn more about evaluating Web sites, many colleges and universities provide sites that help you evaluate Web resources. The following list contains some excellent examples of these evaluation sites:

- Evaluating Quality on the Net—Hope Tillman, Babson College
  www.hopetillman.com/findqual.html
- Critical Web Evaluation—Kurt W. Wagner, William Paterson University of New Jersey
  euphrates.wpunj.edu/faculty/wagnerk/
- Evalation Criteria—Susan Beck, New Mexico State University
  lib.nmsu.edu/instruction/evalcrit.html
- A Student's Guide to Research with the WWW
  www.slu.edu/departments/english/research/
- Evaluating Web Pages: Questions to Ask & Strategies for Getting the Answers
  www.lib.berkeley.edu/TeachingLib/Guides/Internet/EvalQuestions.html

Critical Evaluation Web Sites

WEB SITE AND URL	SOURCE
Critical Thinking in an Online World **www.library.ucsb.edu/untangle/jones.html**	*Paper from "Untangling the Web" 1996*
Educom Review: Information **www.educause.edu/pub/er/review/reviewArticles/31231.html**	*EDUCAUSE Literacy as a Liberal Art (1996 article)*
Evaluating Information Found on the Internet **MiltonsWeb.mse.jhu.edu/research/education/net.html**	*University of Utah Library*
Evaluating Web Sites **www.lib.purdue.edu/InternetEval**	*Purdue University Library*
Evaluating Web Sites **www.lehigh.edu/~inref/guides/evaluating.web.html**	*Lehigh University*
ICONnect: Curriculum Connections Overview **www.ala.org/ICONN/evaluate.html**	*American Library Association's technology education initiative*
Kathy Schrock's ABC's of Web Site Evaluation **www.kathyschrock.net/abceval/**	*Author's Web site*

Kids Pick the best of the Web
"Top 10: Announced"
www.ala.org/news/topkidpicks.html

*American Library Association
initiative underwritten by
Microsoft (1998)*

Resource Selection and Information
Evaluation
**alexia.lis.uiuc.edu/~janicke/
InfoAge.html**

*Univ of Illinois, Champaign-
Urbana (Librarian)*

Testing the Surf: Criteria for Evaluating
Internet Information Sources
**info.lib.uh.edu/pr/v8/n3/
smit8n3.html**

University of Houston Libraries

Evaluating Web Resources
**www2.widener.edu/
Wolfgram-Memorial-Library/
webevaluation/webeval.htm**

Widener University Library

UCLA College Library Instruction:
Thinking Critically about World
Wide Web Resources
**www.library.ucla.edu/libraries/
college/help/critical/**

UCLA Library

UG OOL: Judging Quality on the Internet
**www.open.uoguelph.ca/resources/
skills/judging.html**

University of Guelph

Web Evaluation Criteria
**lib.nmsu.edu/instruction/
evalcrit.html**

*New Mexico State University
Library*

Web Page Credibility Checklist
**www.park.pvt.k12.md.us/academics/
research/credcheck.htm**

Park School of Baltimore

Evaluating Web Sites for Educational
Uses: Bibliography and Checklist
www.unc.edu/cit/guides/irg-49.html

University of North Carolina

Evaluating Web Sites
**www.lesley.edu/library/guides/
research/evaluating_web.html**

Lesley University

Research Navigator Guide: Education

Tip: Can't seem to get a URL to work? If the URL doesn't begin with www, you may need to put the http:// in front of the URL. Usually, browsers can handle URLs that begin with www without the need to type in the "http://" but if you find you're having trouble, add the http://.

Documentation Guidelines for Online Sources

Your Citation for Exemplary Research

There's another detail left for us to handle—the formal citing of electronic sources in academic papers. The very factor that makes research on the Internet exciting is the same factor that makes referencing these sources challenging: their dynamic nature. A journal article exists, either in print or on microfilm, virtually forever. A document on the Internet can come, go, and change without warning. Because the purpose of citing sources is to allow another scholar to retrace your argument, a good citation allows a reader to obtain information from your primary sources, to the extent possible. This means you need to include not only information on when a source was posted on the Internet (if available) but also when you obtained the information.

The two arbiters of form for academic and scholarly writing are the Modern Language Association (MLA) and the American Psychological Association (APA); both organizations have established styles for citing electronic publications.

MLA Style

In the fifth edition of the *MLA Handbook for Writers of Research Papers*, the MLA recommends the following formats:

- **URLs:** URLs are enclosed in angle brackets (<>) and contain the access mode identifier, the formal name for such indicators as "http" or "ftp." If a URL must be split across two lines, break it only after a slash (/). Never introduce a hyphen at the end of the first line. The URL should include all the parts necessary to identify uniquely the file/document being cited.

  `<http://www.csun.edu/~rtvfdept/home/index.html>`

- **An online scholarly project or reference database:** A complete "online reference contains the title of the project or database (underlined); the name of the editor of the project or database (if given); electronic publication information, including version number (if relevant and if not part of the title), date of electronic publication or latest update, and name of any sponsoring institution or organization; date of access; and electronic address.

  The Perseus Project. Ed. Gregory R. Crane. Mar. 1997.
      Department of Classics, Tufts University. 15 June
      1998 <http://www.perseus.tufts.edu/>.

If you cannot find some of the information, then include the information that is available. The MLA also recommends that you print or download electronic documents, freezing them in time for future reference.

- **A document within a scholarly project or reference database:** It is much more common to use only a portion of a scholarly project or database. To cite an essay, poem, or other short work, begin this citation with the name of the author and the title of the work (in quotation marks). Then, include all the information used when citing a complete online scholarly project or reference database, however, make sure you use the URL of the specific work and not the address of the general site.

```
Cuthberg, Lori. "Moonwalk: Earthlings' Finest Hour."
     Discovery Channel Online. 1999. Discovery
     Channel. 25 Nov. 1999 <http://www.discovery.com/
     indep/newsfeatures/moonwalk/challenge.html>.
```

- **A professional or personal site:** Include the name of the person creating the site (reversed), followed by a period, the title of the site (underlined), or, if there is no title, a description such as Home page (such a description is neither placed in quotes nor underlined). Then, specify the name of any school, organization, or other institution affiliated with the site and follow it with your date of access and the URL of the page.

```
Packer, Andy. Home page. 1Apr. 1998 <http://
     www.suu.edu/~students/Packer.htm>.
```

Some electronic references are truly unique to the online domain. These include email, newsgroup postings, MUDs (multiuser domains) or MOOs (multiuser domains, object-oriented), and IRCs (Internet Relay Chats).

Email. In citing email messages, begin with the writer's name (reversed) followed by a period, then the title of the message (if any) in quotations as it appears in the subject line. Next comes a description of the message, typically "Email to," and the recipient (e.g., "the author"), and finally the date of the message.

```
Davis, Jeffrey. "Web Writing Resources." Email to
     Nora Davis. 3 Jan. 2000.
```

```
Sommers, Laurice. "Re: College Admissions
     Practices." Email to the author. 12 Aug. 1998.
```

List Servers and Newsgroups.   In citing these references, begin with the author's name (reversed) followed by a period. Next include the title of the document (in quotes) from the subject line, followed by the words "Online posting" (not in quotes). Follow this with the date of posting. For list servers, include the date of access, the name of the list (if known), and the online address of the list's moderator or administrator. For newsgroups, follow "Online posting" with the date of posting, the date of access, and the name of the newsgroup, prefixed with "news:" and enclosed in angle brackets.

```
Applebaum, Dale. "Educational Variables." Online
    posting. 29 Jan. 1998. Higher Education
    Discussion Group. 30 Jan. 1993
    <jlucidoj@unc.edu>.
```

```
Gostl, Jack. "Re: Mr. Levitan." Online posting.
    13 June 1997. 20 June 1997
    <news:alt.edu.bronxscience>.
```

MUDs, MOOs, and IRCs.   Begin with the name of the speaker(s) followed by a period. Follow with the description and date of the event, the forum in which the communication took place, the date of access, and the online address. If you accessed the MOO or MUD through telnet, your citation might appear as follows:

```
Guest. Personal interview. 13 Aug. 1998.
    <telnet://du.edu:8888>.
```

For more information on MLA documentation style for online sources, check out their Web site at http://www.mla.org/style/sources.htm.

APA Style

The newly revised *Publication Manual of the American Psychological Association* (5th ed.) now includes guidelines for Internet resources. The manual recommends that, at a minimum, a reference of an Internet source should provide a document title or description, a date (either the date of publication or update or the date of retrieval), and an address (in Internet terms, a uniform resource locator, or URL). Whenever possible, identify the authors of a document as well. It's important to remember that, unlike the MLA, the APA does not include temporary or transient sources (e.g., letters, phone calls, etc.) in its "References" page, preferring to handle them in the text. The general suggested format is as follows:

Online periodical:

Author, A. A., Author, B. B., & Author, C. C. (2000). Title of article. *Title of Periodical*, xx, xxxxx. Retrieved month, day, year, from source.

Online document:

Author, A. A. (2000). *Title of work.* Retrieved month, day, year, from source.

Some more specific examples are as follows:

FTP (File Transfer Protocol) Sites. To cite files available for downloading via FTP, give the author's name (if known), the publication date (if available and if different from the date accessed), the full title of the paper (capitalizing only the first word and proper nouns), the date of access, and the address of the FTP site along with the full path necessary to access the file.

Deutsch, P. (1991) Archie: An electronic directory service for the Internet. Retrieved January 25, 2000 from File Transfer Protocol: ftp:// ftp.sura.net/pub/archie/docs/whatis.archie

WWW Sites (World Wide Web). To cite files available for viewing or downloading via the World Wide Web, give the author's name (if known), the year of publication (if known and if different from the date accessed), the full title of the article, and the title of the complete work (if applicable) in italics. Include any additional information (such as versions, editions, or revisions) in parentheses immediately following the title. Include the date of retrieval and full URL (the http address).

Burka, L. P. (1993). A hypertext history of multi-user dungeons. *MUDdex*. Retrieved January 13, 1997 from the World Wide Web: http://www.utopia.com/ talent/lpb/muddex/essay/

Tilton, J. (1995). Composing good HTML (Vers. 2.0.6). Retrieved December 1, 1996 from the World Wide Web: http://www.cs.cmu.edu/~tilt/cgh/

Synchronous Communications (MOOs, MUDs, IRC, etc.). Give the name of the speaker(s), the complete date of the conversation being referenced in parentheses, and the title of the session (if applicable). Next, list the title of the site in italics, the protocol and address (if applicable), and any directions necessary to access the work. Last, list the date of access, followed by the retrieval information. Personal interviews do not need to be listed in the References, but do need to be included in parenthetic references in the text (see the APA *Publication Manual*).

```
Cross, J. (1996, February 27). Netoric's Tuesday
    "cafe: Why use MUDs in the writing classroom?
    MediaMoo. Retrieved March 1, 1996 from File
    Transfer Protocol: ftp://daedalus.com/
    pub/ACW/NETORIC/catalog
```

Gopher Sites.   List the author's name (if applicable), the year of publication, the title of the file or paper, and the title of the complete work (if applicable). Include any print publication information (if available) followed by the protocol (i.e., gopher://). List the date that the file was accessed and the path necessary to access the file.

```
Massachusetts Higher Education Coordinating Council.
    (1994). Using coordination and collaboration to
    address change. Retrieved July 16, 1999 from the
    World Wide Web: gopher://gopher.mass.edu:170/
    00gopher_root%3A%5B_hecc%5D_plan
```

Email, Listservs, and Newsgroups.   Do not include personal email in the list of References. Although unretrievable communication such as email is not included in APA References, somewhat more public or accessible Internet postings from newsgroups or listservs may be included. See the APA *Publication Manual* for information on in-text citations.

```
Heilke, J. (1996, May 3). Webfolios. Alliance for
    Computers and Writing Discussion List. Retrieved
    December 31, 1996 from the World Wide Web:
    http://www.ttu.edu/lists/acw-1/9605/0040.html
```

Other authors and educators have proposed similar extensions to the APA style. You can find links to these pages at:

```
www.psychwww.com/resource/apacrib.htm
```

Remember, "frequently-referenced" does not equate to "correct" "or even "desirable." Check with your professor to see if your course or school has a preference for an extended APA style.

Research Navigator Guide: Education

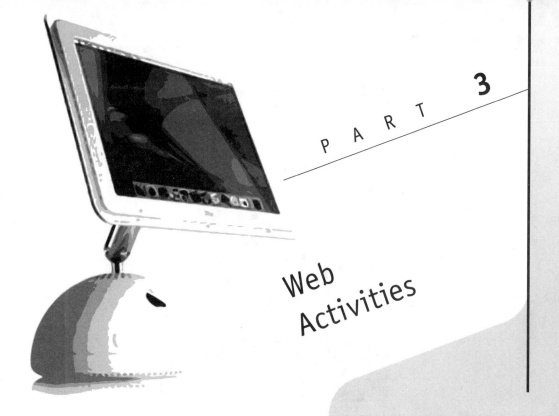

P A R T **3**

Web
Activities

Internet Activities for Education

The following section provides a set of basic exercises to help you become more skilled at finding educational resources on the Web that can help you with your work. Think about each exercise, and then consider how it might make use of some of the other Web sites that are listed throughout this book.

Finding Information Online

There are numerous reference resources available to educators that can help them with their studies and work in the classroom. Each of the following exercises is intended to introduce you to a different type of site.

Exercise: Finding a School Address on the Web

Web 66: The International School Registry Website (**http://web66. coled.umn.edu/schools.html**) is a gateway into thousands of school Web sites across the country and around the world. Visit the site and find a school in your home community. List the name of the school's principal and its main telephone number.

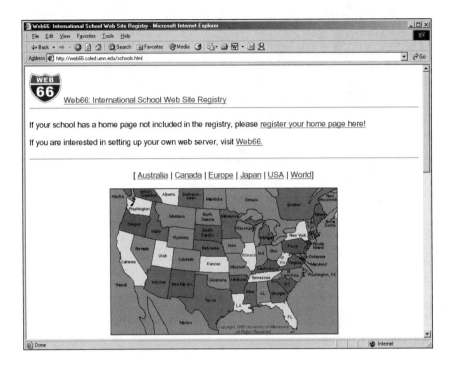

Exercise: Consulting the Encyclopedia Britannica

The Encyclopedia Britannica is now available online (**http://www. britannica.com/**). Not only does it provide excellent general background on almost any topic, but also superb links to Web sites. First, go to **http:// www.britannica.com/** and use the dictionary function at the top of the page to search for a definition of the term "nanotechnology." Next, using the encyclopedia function, search for a topic that interest you. Finally, using the search function, find five Web sites that are available on the topic you have chosen.

Exercise: Consulting an Online Dictionary of Sign Language

Did you know that non-traditional dictionaries and reference sources are available online? One of the best is the Handspeak Dictionary (**http://dww.deafworldweb.org/asl/**). Go to this site and find out what part of the body is pointed to when the sign for "allergy" is made in American Sign Language. Try to imagine how hard it would be to learn signing using a non-multimedia dictionary.

Research Navigator Guide: Education

Kathy Shrock's Guide for Educators

One of the best online resources available for teachers working in the classroom is Kathy Shrock's Guide for Educators (**http://school.discovery.com/schrockguide/**) Web site sponsored by the Discovery Channel. The site not only provides resources for curriculum and professional growth, but also practical tools and materials that will be invaluable for you to use in your classroom. Specialized subject area resources and topics include: Agricultural Education, Business Sources/Grants, Education Resources, Entertainment and Travel, Health, P.E. & Fitness, History and Social Studies, Holiday Celebrations, Internet Information, Kidstuff, Literature/Language Arts, Mathematics, News Sources/Magazines, Organizations/Government, Performing Arts and Music, Reference and Librarians, Science and Technology, Shopping, Special Education Resources, Sports, Vocational Education, Weather Information and Maps, and World Languages/Regions.

Exercise: Researching a Lesson Plan Using Kathy Shrock's Guide

Go to the lesson plan section of Kathy Shrock's Guide (**http://school.discovery.com/lessonplans/**). Find a lesson plan that is appropriate for the grade level and subject you plan to teach. Copy the plan and then modify it to make it fit the needs of the type of school you are, or will

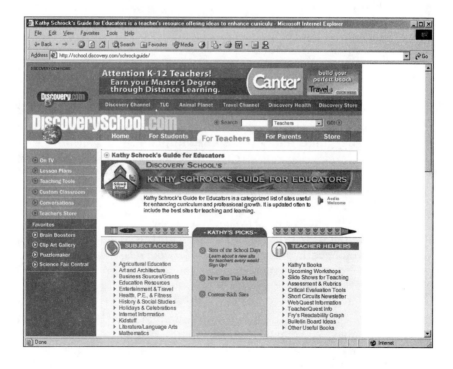

Research Navigator Guide: Education

probably be, working in. Be sure to give credit to the source of the original material.

Exercise: Determining the Readability of a Text Using Kathy Shrock's Guide

Teachers often need to know whether or not materials students are reading are appropriate for their grade level. There are a number of reading scales available that make this possible. Professor Edward Fry, formerly of the Rutgers University Reading Center, created one of the most well known. Go to Kathy Shrock's Guide for Educators to get a copy of Fry's Readability Scale (**http://school.discovery.com/schrockguide/fry/fry.html**). Follow the instructions on how to use it. Then determine the readability of this paragraph, and the one above, or use a selection of text you have chosen yourself.

Exercise: Evaluating Web Sites Using Kathy Shrock's Guide

All Web sites are not created equal. Being able to evaluate which are useful and accurate, and which are not, is an important skill for educators. There are many sites that provide information for reviewing sites. Kathy Shrock's Guide for Educators provides an excellent set of links to software evaluation sites (**http://school.discovery.com/schrockguide/eval.html**). In addition, she also provides Web site evaluation forms for the K–12 level. Use one of her "Critical Evaluation Survey" forms (Elementary, Middle School, Secondary level or Virtual Tour) to analyze a Web site that you could use to in your work as a teacher.

Exercise: Creating a Bulletin Board Using Kathy Shrock's Guide

It's Thanksgiving or Kwanza and you desperately need a bulletin board fast for your class. Go to Kathy Shrock's Guide for Educator's and look at her page "Bulletin Board Ideas" (**http://school.discovery.com/schrockguide/bulletin/elembrd.html**). Plan a bulletin board of your own on special topics (Great Authors, Back to School, Black History Month). Assemble the necessary material from the Web, using not just Shrock's site, but others as well. For example, for a bulletin board on Black History Month go to the Library of Congress's American Memory Project and pull photographs from exhibits like the African-American Odyssey (**http://lcweb2.loc.gov/ammem/aaohtml/**). Assemble all of the materials you need in a notebook or folder. Plan to work in a space measuring 4 × 6 feet. Prepare your materials so that you can arrange the entire bulletin board, even if you don't actually have a classroom. Draw a map of the layout for reference. Keep your bulletin board materials and design as part of your teaching file. You may find it invaluable one rainy day when you need something to brighten up an empty bulletin board in your classroom.

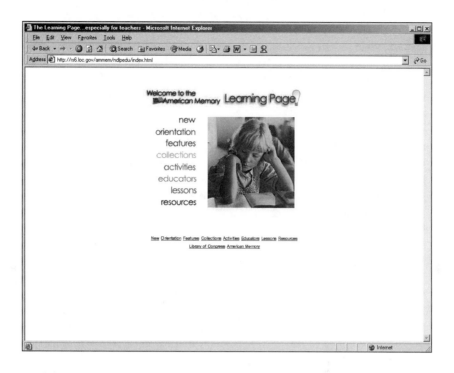

Finding Visual Materials Online

There are many different types of visual sources that you can use in your classroom that can be found online. The following exercises should give you some idea of some of the ways visual sources can be incorporated into your classroom.

Exercise: Using Historical Photographs from the American Memory Collection, Library of Congress

Visual material adds interest to any classroom assignment or lesson. Virtually unlimited visual sources are available on the Internet and World Wide Web that can be used by teachers. Imagine that you are a high school American history teacher doing a unit on the Depression. The American Memory Project at the Library of Congress has literally millions of copyright free photographs available for use. Go to the American Memory Project Learning Page (**http://rs6.loc.gov/ammem/ndlpedu/index.html**) to find how you can access visual materials for use in your classroom. Starting from the Learning Page, see if you can find three photographs that depict economic conditions in the Depression that you could use to illustrate a lecture or discussion. Suggestions: Check the "15 Popular Requests From the FSA-OWI Collection" (**http://memory.loc.gov/ammem/fsahtml/fatop1. html**) for some of the most well known photographs from the Depression that are included in the collections at the Library of Congress. To save or copy a photograph, drag your mouse over the image and click on your mouse. A sidebar menu will appear that you will allow you to copy the jpeg or gif image on your computer screen or save it to your computer. Larger images can be downloaded following instructions from the Library of Congress Web site.

Exercise: Finding Clip Art Sources Online

The Microsoft Corporation provides an extraordinary collection of clip art that can be used for free. Go to the Microsoft Design Gallery Live (**http://dgl.microsoft.com/**) to find images of each of the following: 1. a silhouette of a teacher; 2. an image of the Statue of Liberty; 3. a picture of Abraham Lincoln; and, 4. the image of a frog.

Finding Out About Current Issues Using the Internet

There are numerous resources available on the Internet to find out about contemporary educational issues and problems. The following exercises will help you become familiar with just a couple of resources that will keep you current on issues affecting education.

Exercise: Learning About Current Issues at Union Web Sites

Professional organizations such as the National Education Association (**http://www.nea.org/**) and the American Federation of Teachers (**http://www.aft.org/index.htm**) have excellent Web pages that address current issues in education. Go the NEA's issues page and find out what research has determined is the optimum class size for teaching (**http://www.nea.org/issues/**). Go to the AFT's issues (**http://www.aft.org/issues/meritpay/index.html**) page and find the answer to the question, "Has merit pay succeeded for teachers in past?"

Exercise: Reading Education Week

Want to find out what is going on at the state and local level in terms of education? There are few better sources than *Education Week* (**http://www.edweek.org/**), the country's main weekly newspaper dealing with educational issues. Visit their electronic Web site and summarize, in a brief paragraph, an article you think is interesting or relevant to your potential work as a teacher.

Using the Web to go on an Electronic Field Trip

Taking a field trip is now possible for classes with just the click of a mouse. The Tower of London (**http://www.tower-of-london.com/**), the

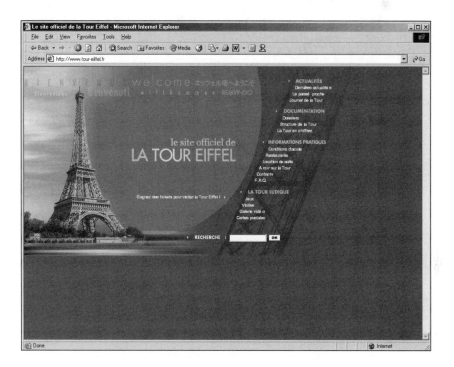

United Nations (**http://www.un.org/**), and the Eiffel Tower (**http://www.tour-eiffel.fr/**) can easily be accessed on the Web.

Exercise: Taking a Field Trip to Paris

Go to the Eiffel Tower home page (**http://www.tour-eiffel.fr/**), click on the historical page and find out when and why the tower was built. Then go on to other sites including the Louvre (**http://www.louvre.fr/louvrea.htm**) and the great cathedral of Notre Dame (**http://www2.art.utah.edu/cathedral/paris.html**). Select materials you could use in a bulletin board display or as part of a class project.

Exercise: Visiting a Museum

It is hard to find a major museum that does not have a Web site. Visit the Smithsonian Institution in Washington, D.C. and tour its museums (**http://www.si.edu/portal/lt3-infocenter_museumguide.htm**). Explain which one of them you like the best, and which would be most helpful to you in your work as a teacher.

Research Navigator Guide: Education

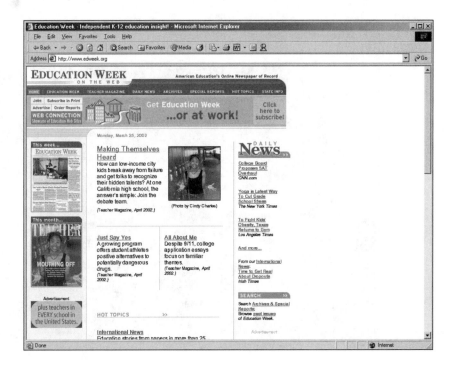

Job Searches

The Internet and World Wide Web are some of the best places for you to search for a job. The following exercises will help you become more familiar with where teaching jobs are posted and how you can get networked.

Exercise: Searching for Jobs

Education Week is the country's main weekly newspaper dealing with educational issues. Its electronic site is available at: (**http://www. edweek.org/**). Besides educational issues, the Education Week Web site provides other types of information, including listings of teaching jobs around the country. Go to their job listings page (**http://www.edweek. org/jobs.cfm**) and find a dream job for yourself either in your local community, or elsewhere in the country. Copy the material for the job listing and print it off.

Exercise: Visiting a Job Site Gateway

There are several Web sites available that make it easier to search for teaching jobs online including K–12 Jobs.com (**http://www.k12jobs. com/**). Check out this and other similar sites by typing into a search en-

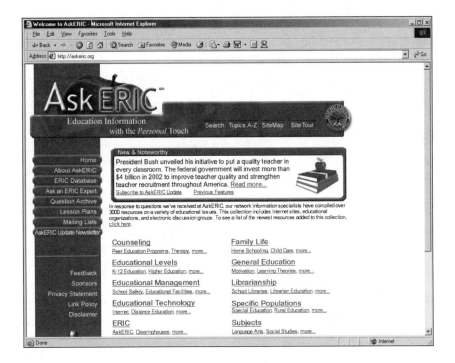

gine "Teaching Jobs." Also go to your local school district's Web site and see what jobs are posted and the procedures for applying.

Exercise: Ask ERIC about Certification

Ask Eric (**http://askeric.org/**) is a service of the Federal Government that provides answers to educational questions asked by the researchers, teachers and the general public. There is a useful Frequently Asked Questions (FAQs) page. Consult the page that answers questions about teacher certification and the requirements that are found throughout the country. Research the requirements in your state. Make a list of the basic requirements necessary for you to be certified in your state, or the state you plan to teach in.

Search Engines

Using search engines critically is essential if you are to get the maximum benefit possible out of the Internet. The following exercises will help you become more familiar with the possibilities and limitations of many search engines.

Exercise: Searching the Internet for Education Resources

Different search engines yield different results. Go to the University of California Library site "Internet Search Tool Details" (**http://sunsite. berkeley.edu/help/searchdetails.html**) and see what types of results you get exploring the same subject using different search engines. Search for a subject of your choosing ("Piaget and Education," "School Vouchers," "School Violence" are examples). What happens when you use a search engine like AltaVista versus HotBot or Excite?

Exercise: Using a Meta Search Engine

With a meta-search engine, you submit keywords in its search box, and it transmits your search simultaneously to different search engines and their databases of Web pages. It then merges the results for your review. You can learn more about Meta Search Engines at the University of California at Berkley's site Meta-Search Engines (**http://www.lib.berkeley.edu/ TeachingLib/Guides/Internet/MetaSearch.html**). Try a traditional search using a meta-search engine like Google (**www.google.com**) and compare the results to using another search engine like Excite (**http:// www.excite.com/**).

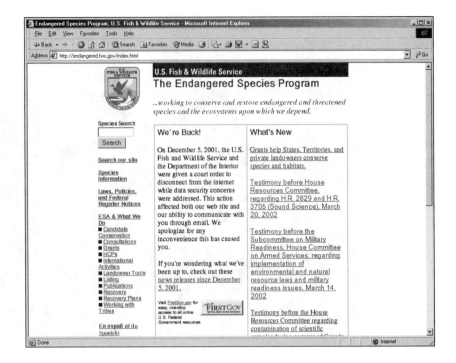

General Research

There are a lot of general research activities that you can conduct from your desk using resources on the Internet and World Wide Web. Complete the following exercises to get a sense of a few of the possibilities.

Exercise: Finding Out About Endangered Animals

Go to the Endangered Species Web site for the U.S. Fish and Wildlife Service (**http://endangered.fws.gov/index.html**). Use the site's search engine and find the status for the California Condor and the Higgins' eye Pearlymussel ("Endangered" or "Threatened"). What is the status of each?

Exercise: Finding Newbery Award Titles

The Newbery Medal is named for eighteenth-century British publisher John Newbery, and is awarded each year by the American Library Association. It recognizes what they believe to be that year's most distinguished contribution to American literature for children. Go to the Newbery Award Web site (**http://www.ala.org/alsc/newbery.html**) and find what 1972 book with a reference to a rodent in its title, won the award for the best book of the year.

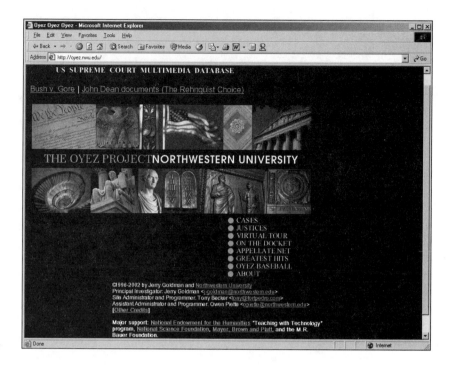

Exercise: Researching a Supreme Court Case on Education

There are several excellent Web sites that deal with the Supreme Court and its major cases. Go to the Web site Oyez Oyez Oyez (**http://oyez. nwu.edu.**) or the Supreme Court Collection (**http://supct.law.cornell. edu/supct/**) and look up the case of *West Virginia State Board of Ed. v. Barnette* (1943). Find out what it was that the students in a West Virginia school did not have to do because of their religious beliefs.

Exercise: Using Data from the Census Bureau

The U.S. Census Bureau (**http://www.census.gov**) is an outstanding source of both contemporary and historical data of interest to educators. Go to the home page of the Census Bureau and find out the current population of the United States and of the World.

Exercise: Mapping Your Neighborhood

The U.S. Census Bureau Web site includes a service that makes it possible for you to find a map of any address in the country and to obtain general demographic information on the area mapped. Go to the Bureau's American Fact Finder Page (**http://factfinder.census.gov/servlet/ basicfactsservlet**) and download or print out a map for where you live.

Research Navigator Guide: Education

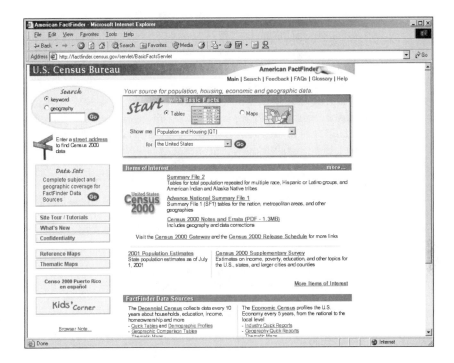

Exercise: Calculating Inflation

Various inflation calculators can be found on the Internet. Go to NASA's inflation calculator (**http://www.jsc.nasa.gov/bu2/inflate.html**) and determine how much you would have to earn today to have the equivalent buying power of $10,000 in 1980.

Special Internet Activities for Multicultural Education

Online Examples

There is much to investigate in Multicultural education by engaging students in selected WWW activities. This section is intended to provide Web-based examples of teaching and learning about Multiculturalism in the Pre-K–16 classroom. The following examples provide URL's, which demonstrate practical applications of Internet resources.

To acquire an overview of Multicultural education proceed by locating six WWW activity sites. Cite selected "mega Internet sites," which may be of value to your study of Multiculturalism. These sites should be age appropriate for the student of Multiculturalism. Yes, it is appropriate to visit the authors' selected URL's. But also feel free to use several search engines to locate Multicultural sites. Explain your rationale for the selection of each of these six "mega-sites." Each of these sites will have multiple links and student activities. Why are some Multicultural sites informative and educational, while other sites may simply promote various view points. What are the qualities of an academically appropriate site? In evaluating a site for educational use, what are the important qualities that the site should exhibit?

_____

_____

_____

_____

Allyn and Bacon has developed a powerful Web site at **http://www.ablongman.com.** Visit this site to locate possible Multicultural college textbooks and/or other college textbooks. How have these textbooks been supplemented by the "digital connection?" Why would professors and students seek texts that have Digital and Web based supplemental materi-

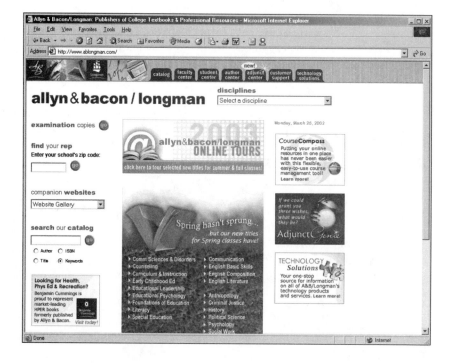

als. Explain how this companion text, *Multiculturalism on the Web* enriches student experiences in critical thinking activities.

_____

_____

_____

_____

_____

_____

_____

_____

Allyn and Bacon has provided *Multiculturalism on the Web* as a supplement text to assist research and critical thinking experiences. Explain how this companion text, *Multiculturalism on the Web* enriches student experiences in critical thinking activities. In visiting the many recommended Multicultural sites be certain to apply the following criteria in determining valid Multicultural learning experiences:

- Does the site provide interactive learning activities?
- Is the site objective?
- Does the site provide for a variety of learning styles?
- Does the site provide additional links?
- Does the site provide for critical examination of divergent perspectives?
- Does the site provide for collaborative activities?

_____

_____

_____

_____

_____

_____

Multiculturalism consists of several subcategories. In a later section the authors cite selected URL's for specific subcategories of Multiculturalism. Use a search engine to locate three activity based WWW sites in the subcategories of **Age, Religion, Class, Exceptionalities, Gender, Inclusion, Language, Ethnicity, Sexual Orientation, and Teaching Resources.**

- Does the site invite diverse perspective, or does it offer a single viewpoint?

- Are supporting sources biased or unbiased?
- Does the site provide forums for discussion of divergent perspectives?
- Is the site's author qualified as a Multicultural expert?
- Is there any evidence of quality control?

_____

_____

_____

_____

_____

_____

Intercultural Email Classroom Connections

http://www.iecc.org

IECC (Intercultural Email Classroom Connections) is a free service to help teachers link with partners in other countries and cultures for email classroom and project exchanges. Since its creation in 1992, IECC has distributed over 28,000 requests for email partnerships. At last count, more than

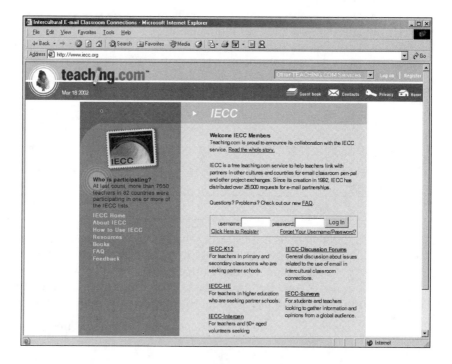

7650 teachers in 82 countries were participating in one or more of the IECC list. This site is maintained by St. Olaf College is a four-year liberal arts college located one hour south of Minneapolis, Minnesota. A school of approximately 2,900 students, St. Olaf College emphasizes a global perspective; it fosters this through a variety of international and off-campus study programs as well as by hosting the the IECC mailing lists. Some special features of this site follow:

- IECC-HE (for Higher Ed)
  IECC-HE is intended for teachers seeking partner classrooms for international and cross-cultural email exchanges with institutions of higher education.
- IECC (for K–12)
  IECC is intended for teachers seeking partner classrooms for international and cross-cultural email exchanges. This list is not for discussion or for people seeking individual penpals.
- IECC-INTERGEN
  IECC-INTERGEN is intended for teachers and "50+ Volunteers" seeking partners for intergenerational email exchanges.
- IECC-PROJECTS
  IECC-PROJECTS is an electronic mailing list where teachers may announce or request help with specific classroom projects that involve email, internationally or cross-culturally.
- IECC-SURVEYS
  IECC-SURVEYS is a forum for students (and teachers) to post requests for assistance on projects, surveys, and questionaires. This differs from the IECC-PROJECTS mailing list, which is intended only for teachers seeking classroom partners on specific projects.
- IECC-DISCUSSION
  IECC-DISCUSSION is intended for general discussion about the applications and implications of intercultural email classroom connections.

How can these services promote Multicultural understanding? Why or why not would these services be productive for the students in your Multicultural course?

_____

_____

_____

_____

_____

_____

_____

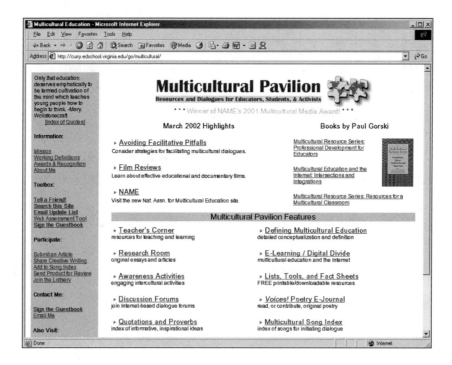

Multicultural Pavilion

`http://curry.edschool.Virginia.EDU/go/multicultural/`

This is a mega-site that has provides numerous features:

- The site provide interactive learning activities.
- The the site is objective and scholarly.
- The site provides many additional links.
- The site provides for critical examination of divergent perspectives.
- The site provides for collaborative activities.

Click on the Awareness Activities. Continue to explore several of these activities.

1. Why are "Icebreakers" important in dealing with Multicultural issues?

_____

_____

_____

2. Why is self-reflection important to understanding prejudice and discrimination?

_____

_____

_____

3. Click on the Boy and Girl Pieces. What critical analysis is necessary to understand this section of the site?

_____

_____

_____

4. Why is the "exchanging stories—names" section a powerful exercise? Be careful to note the Points to remember:

- Because some individuals will include very personal information, some may be hesitant to read them, even in the small groups.
- It is sometimes effective in such situations for facilitators to share their stories first. If you make yourself vulnerable, others will be more comfortable doing the same.
- Be sure to allow time for everyone to be able to speak, whether reading their stories or sharing them from memory.
- When everyone has shared, ask participants how it felt to share their stories. Why is this activity important? What did you learn?

_____

_____

_____

_____

_____

_____

_____

free! The Freedom Forum Online

`http://www.freedomforum.org`

This site is an interactive daily newsletter, which discusses issues related to freedom of religion and other first amendment rights.

Research Navigator Guide: Education

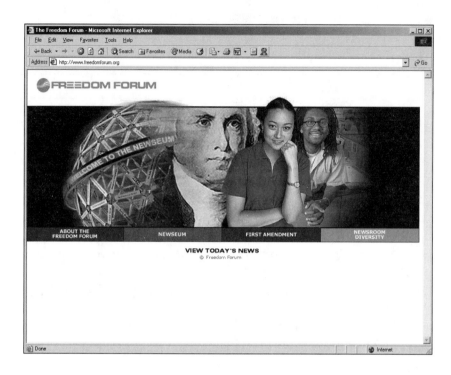

Cite three current issues involving the **FIRST AMENDMENT** and state your position on each of these.

1. _____

_____

_____

_____

2. _____

_____

_____

_____

3. _____

_____

_____

_____

Click on the **NEWSROOM DIVERSITY.**

Cite three current issues involving from **NEWSROOM DIVERSITY** and state your position on each of these.

1. _____

_____

_____

_____

2. _____

_____

_____

_____

3. _____

_____

_____

_____

Intercultural Activities

http://www.mhhe.com/socscience/education/multi/
activities.html

What ground rules should be established in talking about Multicultural issues? Why would you agree or disagree that the following set of ground rules may or may not be important in dealing with Multicultural issues?

- Listen actively—respect others when they are talking.
- Speak from your own experience instead of generalizing ("I" instead of "they," "we," and "you").
- Practice timely attendance.
- Do not be afraid to respectfully challenge one another by asking questions, but refrain from personal attacks—focus on ideas.
- Participate to the fullest of your ability—community growth depends on the inclusion of every individual voice.
- Instead of invalidating somebody else's story with your own spin on their experience, share your own story and experience.
- The goal is not to agree—it is about hearing and exploring divergent perspectives.
- Be conscious of body language and nonverbal responses—they can be as disrespectful as words.

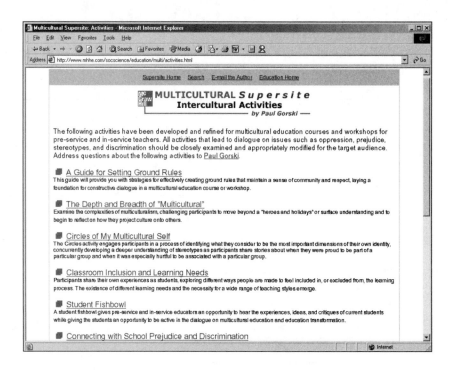

Click on the Multicultural Awareness Quiz. The Multicultural Awareness Quiz illustrates how our perceptions of reality, and the "facts" we are taught through the media, the education system, and other sources of information, are often limited in depth or simply wrong. Students take a multiple choice quiz with questions relating to race, gender, and socioeconomic class, then discuss the correct answers and their own misperceptions.

_____

_____

_____

_____

The Nacirema

`http://www.beadsland.com/FCT/nacirema/html/shome/`

Educators and Multicultural educators have considered the study of the Nacirema as a classic example of introductory activities and literature for decades. The authors have used this example in public school teaching for over three decades. Have students read aloud the article, the Nacirema.

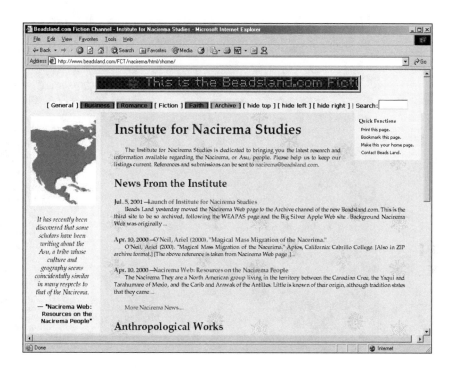

At what point do students begin to understand the article?

_____

_____

_____

What is the central hypothesis of this article?

_____

_____

_____

How might this article be considered exemplary to Multiculturalism?

_____

_____

_____

What are three other articles that provide similar examples to the Nacirema?

_____

_____

_____

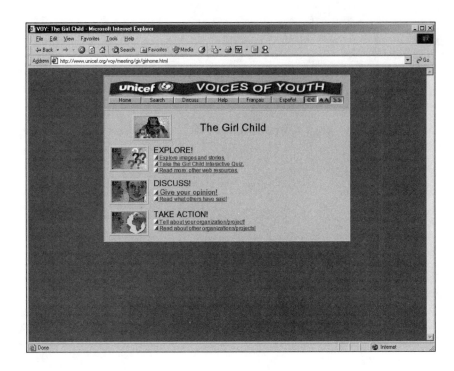

The Girl Child

`http://www.unicef.org/voy/meeting/gir/girhome.html`

This site focuses on providing information about discrimination against girls at all ages of development.

1. Take the Girl Child Interactive Quiz.

2. Cite five factors, which influence parental behavior from this quiz.

_____

_____

_____

_____

_____

3. Were there any issues, which conflicted with your beliefs?

_____

_____

_____

4. Click on the button, compose your opinion, and email your opinion.

Research Navigator Guide: Education

Special Education Resources on the Internet (SERI)

`http://seriweb.com/`

This mega-site provides interconnections to general information on disabilities as well as on specific disabilities. Resources are provided to location legal information, associations and national professional, support, advocacy and discussion groups, as well as products and services. Informative resources for parents and educators and assistance in inclusion and transition are also provided.

1. Click on Selected Books related to Special Education. Cite six books, which have special interest to you.

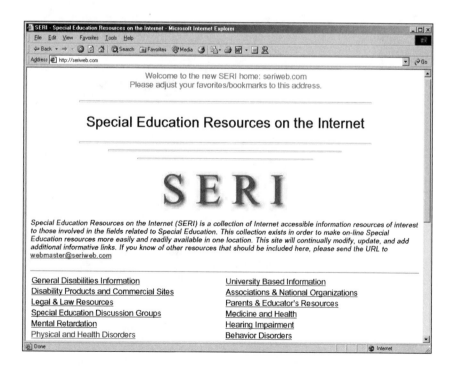

2. Summarize the content of one or two of the books that are of particular interest to the user A search engine may assist with this review. Why are these particular books or particular interest to you?

_____

_____

_____

_____

Explore Linguistics!

`http://logos.uoregon.edu/explore/`

This site is devoted to the study of language and linguistics.

1. Define the concept of sociolinguistics.

_____

_____

_____

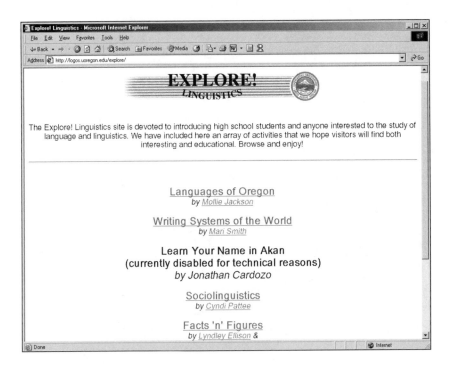

2. How does the film, *What Women Want* relate to the concept of socio-linguistics?

_____

_____

_____

3. What evidence supports the hypothesis that men and women speak differently?

_____

_____

_____

4. Cite five current books, which explore the differences in gender and linguistics

_____

_____

_____

Working Definition of Gender Equity in Education

http://www.edc.org/WomensEquity

This Web site offers a working definition of gender equity in education. These activities are intended to explore an individual's gender identity as related to expectations of others and the influences of the media.

Click on the Publications Section. Cite six books, which have special interest to you. Summarize the content of one or two books. A search engine may assist with this review. Why do these books have special interest to you?

_____

_____

_____

_____

_____

_____

_____

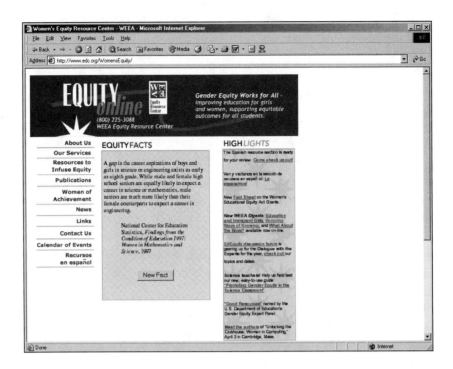

Gender Equity in Education: Additional Resources

`http://www.ed.gov/offices/ODS/g-equity.html`

Multiple links to organizations and resources supporting equity in education for females and other underrepresented groups.

Define the concept, Title IX. Why was this federal legislation necessary? In what manner is Title IX being upheld or ignored in your educational institution? Cite five other resources form this Web site that you would be interested in investigating.

_____

_____

_____

_____

_____

_____

_____

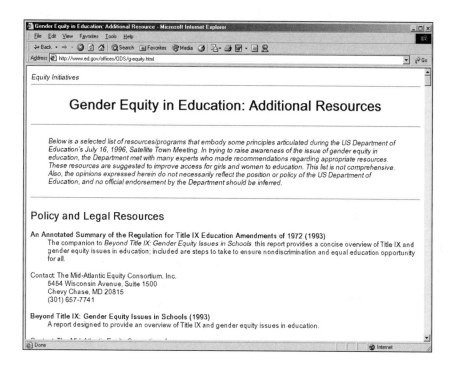

Men's Issues Links

`http://www.abs-comptech.com/frn/menissue.html`

An electronic link to Web sites on men's issues, such as: dispelling gender myths, inequities in the judicial against men, etc. Also provides links to men's magazines and organizations.

1. **Click on why Boys Hide Their Emotions.** This is an ABC news transcript. List five issues, which concern you from this transcript. What is your reaction to this transcript?

_____

_____

_____

_____

2. **Click on the Divorce Reform Page.** Cite five ways in which divorce differs in the fifty states.

_____

_____

_____

Research Navigator Guide: Education

```
Men's Issues - Microsoft Internet Explorer                                    _ |□| x
File   Edit   View   Favorites   Tools   Help                                     ※
← Back  ▾  →  ▾  ⊗  ⊠  ⌂   ⊗ Search  ⌹ Favorites  ⊛ Media  ⊚  ⊠ ▾  ⊜  ⊠ ▾  ⊟  ⊠
Address  ⊠ http://www.abs-comptech.com/lrn/menissue.html                    ▾  ⌀ Go
```

Men's/Family Issues

Features - Online Books

Father Facts - an excellent resource by Dr. Wade Horn.

Bachelor Parents and Their Functional Families
a guide to successful parenting for the single father

The Garbage Generation

The Head of the Medusa

Anti-Feminism -- Discussion and Resources -A large archive of resources starts here. Surprise! :-)

The Anti-Feminist Page - Books and links to a small part of the anti-feminist web. Most anti-feminists are
not for women only ("ism"="for" + "femin"="woman"), but to children and men, also.

A Man's Life
A mainstream and up-beat men's issues magazine.

The Backlash!
The Backlash! is a magazine of men's issues administered by Rod Van Mechelen. His Web site hosts many men's rights
commentaries and much information.

```
⊠ Done                                                          ⊛ Internet
```

3. **Click on Model legislative provisions on pre-marital education or training page.** What reaction do you have to this proposed
   legislation?

Rationale and Guidelines for Teaching about Religion

`http://www.ncss.org/standards/positions/religion.html`

The National Council for the Social Studies (NCSS) states that knowledge
about religion is a characteristic of an educated person. They maintain that
it is absolutely necessary for understanding and living in a world of diver-

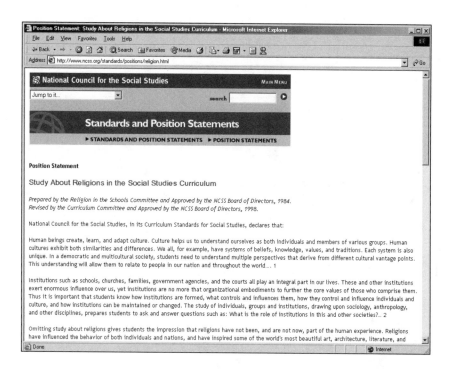

sity. NCSS provides guidelines and suggestion for how this study can take place in the public school system.

1. Why is study about religion important in the public school curriculum?

_____

_____

_____

2. Summarize the Religious Liberty clauses of the First Amendment to the Constitution, which provide the civic framework for teaching about religion in the public school

_____

_____

_____

3. Explain the quote, "The school's approach to religion is *academic,* not *devotional.*"

_____

_____

_____

4. How can role-playing and outside speakers promote the study about religion in the public school curriculum?

_____

_____

_____

Women of NASA

http://quest.arc.nasa.gov/women/intro.html

The Women of NASA resource was developed to encourage more young women to inspire their interest and provide support to pursue careers in math, science and technology. Specific ideas to include Women of NASA on teaching are at: **http://quest.arc.nasa.gov/women/teachingtips.html**

1. Click on teaching tips
2. Click on Women of NASA Occupations Chat Lesson
3. List and download the "supplies" necessary for this lesson

_____

_____

_____

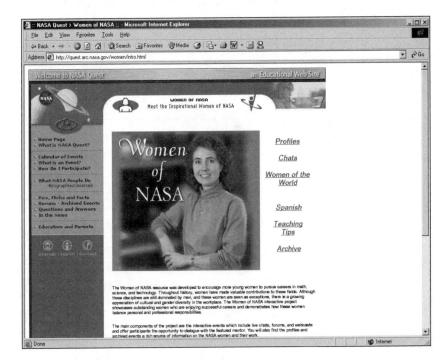

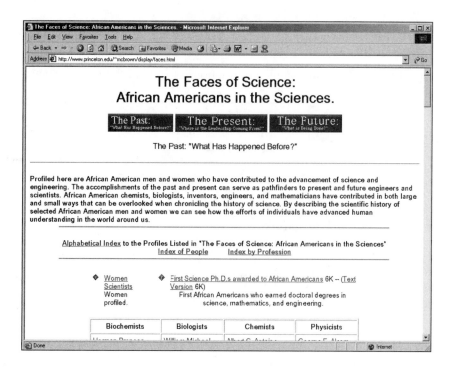

4. Why was this an effective means of teaching?

_____

_____

_____

The Faces of Science: African Americans in the Sciences

`http://www.princeton.edu/~mcbrown/display/faces.html`

This Web page lists African American men and women who have contributed to the advancement of science and engineering. African American chemists, biologists, inventors, engineers, and mathematicians have contributed in both large and small ways that can be overlooked when chronicling the history of science. This site may offer great encouragement to future generations.

1. Select five profiles of African American Scientists.

_____

_____

_____

2. Relate important contributions of each of these five scientists.

_____

_____

_____

_____

_____

Black Inventors

http://www.freep.com/blackhistory/bhinvent/index.htm

A Web site dedicated to the many contributions of African-American inventors and their inventions.

1. Select five profiles of African American Inventors.

_____

_____

_____

_____

_____

2. Relate important contributions of each of these five inventors.

_____

_____

_____

_____

_____

_____

_____

_____

_____

_____

_____

_____

_____

_____

_____

Research Navigator Guide: Education

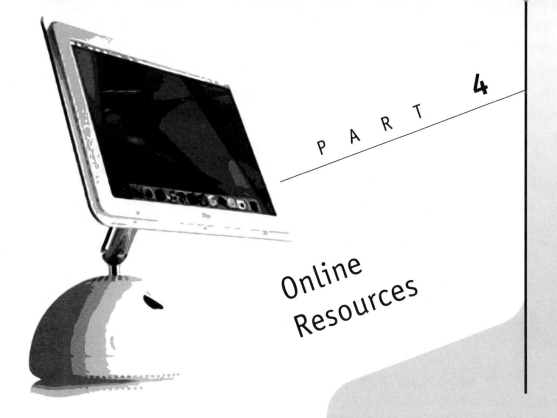

P A R T   4

Online
Resources

Internet Sites Useful in Education

Introduction to Education

The Web is an ideal place to learn about schools and teaching. Among the best starting points to research accreditation issues and requirements for entering the profession is the National Council for the Accreditation of Teacher Education (NCATE).

National Council for the Accreditation of Teacher Education

`http://ncate.org/`

Certification requirements vary across different states. To find out what is required in each state visit the following gateway site at the University of Kentucky. It will take you to the appropriate Web site to learn about certification requirements for each state throughout the country.

50 States' Certification Requirements

`http://www.uky.edu/Education/TEP/usacert.html`

You can connect to other teachers for help on lesson plans, professional planning, and similar types of issues by connecting to Teacher Talk at Indiana University:

Teacher Talk

`http://education.indiana.edu/cas/tt/tthmpg.html`

Teachers Helping Teachers describes itself as a service that provides "basic teaching tips to inexperienced teachers; ideas that can be immediately implemented into the classroom . . . new ideas in teaching methodologies for all teachers . . . (and) a forum for experienced teachers to share their expertise and tips with colleagues around the world."

Teachers Helping Teachers

`http://www.pacificnet.net/~mandel/index.html`

Social and Cultural Foundations

The U.S. Department of Education includes extensive research reports and compilations of data for many topics you may need to explore in the social foundations area. Who are dropouts? What are the employment projections for teachers? What is the representation of different racial and minority groups in the public schools? How many private school students are there in the United States? These are just a few examples of the type of information that is available.

U.S. Department of Education

`http://www.ed.gov/`

For national attitudes and opinions about schools and American society in general, visit the Gallup Organization:

Gallup Organization

`http://www.gallup.com/`

Information on toleration, Civil Rights and equity issues can be found at:

Museum of Tolerance

`http://www.wiesenthal.com/mot`

Research Navigator Guide: Education

Another good site for Civil Rights is the:

National Civil Rights Museum

```
http://www.civilrightsmuseum.org
```

An excellent set of links for different aspects of the Afro-American experience can be found at:

The Universal Black Pages

```
http://www.ubp.com/
```

For links on Chicano and Latino culture visit:

Chicano/Latino Net

```
http://latino.sscnet.ucla.edu/
```

Native American links are available at:

Native Web

```
http://www.nativeweb.org/
```

For general sources on diversity and education visit:

University of Maryland Diversity Database

```
http://www.inform.umd.edu/EdRes/Topic/Diversity/
```

Excellent materials on gender equity can be found at:

The American Association of University Women

```
http://www.aauw.org/
```

Make sure to connect to the following page at the American Association of University Women for educational equity materials:

Research on Gender Equity

```
http://www.aauw.org/2000/research.html
```

Other gender equity resources can be found at:

Equity Online

```
http://www.edc.org/WomensEquity/
```

Use the following site to learn about population trends (how many people teach, who goes to school, and the like). You will also be able to find census data for your own community.

U.S. Census Bureau

http://www.census.gov

The country's only museum dedicated exclusively to the work of women can be found at:

The National Museum of Women in the Arts

http://www.nmwa.org

Psychological Foundations

Many of the Web-based resources you are most likely to be interested in for the field of educational psychology can be found at psychology gateway Web sites such as:

Brown University, Department of Cognitive and Linguistic Sciences

http://www.cog.brown.edu/

Individual figures important in educational psychology and psychology can be researched. For example, background on the Swiss psychologist Jean Piaget is available at:

The Jean Piaget Society

http://www.piaget.org/

Look specifically at the subpage entitled:

A Short Biography of Jean Piaget

http://www.piaget.org/biography/biog.html

To learn about the Russian constructivist Lev Vygotsky, you can visit:

The Virtual Faculty's Second Project

http://www.massey.ac.nz/~ALock/virtual/project2.htm

School psychology resources can be found online at:

School Psychology Resources Online

http://mail.bcpl.lib.md.us/~sandyste/school_psych.html

Special Education

The Web provides exceptional resources for those interested in different areas of special education. Separate sites can be found for various areas of special needs, as well as on the use of computers by individuals with special needs.

Apple's The Disability Connection

`http://www.apple.com/disability/`

An excellent gateway site for both products and Web sites that deal with disabilities.

Learning Disabilities Association

`http://www.ldanatl.org/`

The Learning Disabilities Association of America purpose is to advance the education and general welfare individuals who have disabilities of a perceptual, conceptual, or coordinative nature.

Blind Links

`http://www.seidata.com/~marriage/rblind.html`

An excellent gateway site for those interested in blind resources on the Internet.

C.H.A.D.D. Online: Children and Adults with Attention Deficit Disorder

`http://www.chadd.org/`

Extensive resources on Attention Deficit Disorder and Hyperactivity Disorder.

Down Syndrome

`http://www.nas.com/downsyn/`

Major resources compiled by experts on Down syndrome.

Family Village

`http://www.familyvillage.wisc.edu/`

This site brings together information, resources, and communication opportunities on the Internet for persons with cognitive and other disabilities, their families, and service and support providers.

Research Navigator Guide: Education

Jerome and Deborah's Big Page of Special Education Links

http://www.mts.net/~jgreenco/special.html

Web links for a wide range of Special Education sources.

LD Online

http://www.ldonline.org/

Extensive Web site providing information on Learning Disabilities.

The Council for Exceptional Children's Home Page

http://www.cec.sped.org/

The main research groups in the country dealing with special populations in education.

The National Information Center for Children and Youth with Disabilities

http://www.nichcy.org/

The government's main site for children and young people with disabilities.

Sign Language Dictionary

http://www/bconnex.net/~randys

A remarkable animated dictionary of deaf sign language.

Society for the Autistically Handicapped

http://www.autismuk.com/

Information resource site dealing with all aspects of autism.

Special Education Resources (University of Virginia)

http://curry.edschool.virginia.edu/go/specialed/

An excellent general collection of resources on people and resources in Special Education.

U.S. Department of Justice American with Disabilities Acts

http://www.usdoj.gov/crt/ada/adahom1.htm

Legal information for people with special needs can be found at this site.

Gifted Education

As with the more general field of special education, gifted education is well represented on the Internet. Check the following sites:

Yahoo! Gifted Youth Links

http://www.yahoo.com/education/k_12/gifted_youth/

Resources about the gifted and talented on the Internet.

Education: Gifted and Talented Students

http://www.kidsource.com/kidsource/pages/
ed.gifted.html

A useful gateway site.

Johns Hopkins University, Center for Talented Youth (CTY)

http://www.jhu.edu/~gifted/

One of the country's major sites for researching the gifted and talented.

Multicultural Education

Multicultural education sources on the Internet and World Wide Web include a wide range of sites, from information on historical figures such as Martin Luther King to sources on Native American people. A good place to begin is the Web site "Walk a Mile in My Shoes:"

Walk a Mile in My Shoes: Multicultural Curriculum Resources

http://www.wmht.org/trail/explor02.htm

Sources on Latino culture can be found at:

Latin American Network Information Center

http://lanic.utexas.edu

Another useful site dealing with diversity is the University of Virginia School of Education's Multicultural Pavilion:

Multicultural Pavilion

http://curry.edschool.Virginia.edu/go/multicultural/

Interesting Native American sites can be found at:

Native American Indian Resources

`http://www.kstrom.net/isk/mainmenu.html`

Material on Native American literature can be found at:

Indigenous People's Literature

`http://www.indigenouspeople.org/natlit/natlit.htm`

Computers and Education

Technology and education is a hot topic. Teachers will increasingly use computers in their instruction, particularly as machines and software become cheaper and more widely available. Some good Web sites to check out include:

Technology Education Home Page

`http://ed1.eng.ohio-state.edu/`

Ohio State's resource site on technology and instruction.

International Society for Technology in Education

`http://www.iste.org/`

The major international organization dealing with technology in education.

World Wide Web for Teachers

`http://www.4teachers.org/home/index.shtml`

A Webzine for teachers interested in using technology in their classrooms.

Edutech: Online Resources for Education and Technology

`http://agora.unige.ch/tecfa/edutech/welcome.html`

Explore major issues on technology and education by themes at this site.

If you want to learn about the history of the Internet and World Wide Web, a good place to begin is:

Historical Timeline of the Internet

`http://www.zakon.org/robert/internet/timeline`

For information on how widespread the Internet is see:

Cyber Atlas

`http://cyberatlas.internet.com/`

Information about Internet filters and protecting children can be found at:

Internet Safety for Kids

`http://www.ou.edu/oupd/kidsafe/warn_kid.htm`

A good guide for surfing the Internet safely for children is:

Tips for Safer Surfing

`http://www.safesurf.com/lifegard.htm`

To learn about using Internet search engines visit the following site:

Internet Search Engine Details

`http://sunsite.berkeley.edu/help/searchdetails.html`

Research-It provides excellent search systems in a wide range of subject areas.

Research-It!

`http://www.itools.com/research-it/`

Children's Literature and Language Arts

An excellent starting point for learning about children's literature on the Web is:

Carol Hurst's Children's Literature Site

`http://www.carolhurst.com/`

Another good resource for learning about children's books is:

The Children's Literature Web Guide

`http://www.ucalgary.ca/~dkbrown/index.html`

You can go online to ask well-known children's authors questions by visiting the following site:

"Ask the Author"

`http://ipl.sils.umich.edu/youth/AskAuthor/`

Research Navigator Guide: Education

Other Web sites on children's literature, folklore, and mythology include:

Classics for Young People

http://www.ucalgary.ca/~dkbrown/storclas.html

Full text sources online for classic children's stories and books.

Kindred Spirits (L. M. Mongomery Institute)

http://www.upei.ca/~lmmi/

A research site devoted to the author of *Anne of Green Gables*.

Laura Ingalls Wilder Home Page

http://webpages.marshall.edu/~irby1/laura.htmlx

Laura Ingalls Wilder fans will particularly appreciate this site.

The Little Red Riding Hood Project

http://www-dept.usm.edu/~engdept/lrrh/lrrhhome.htm

Everything about this classic fairy tale.

Newbery Award Home Page

http://www.ala.org/alsc/newbery.html

The home page for the United State's major children's book award.

Grimm's Fairy Tales

http://www.cs.cmu.edu/~spok/grimmtmp/

Full text versions of the Grimm tales.

Winnie the Pooh and Friends

http://worldkids.net/pooh/welcome.html

An award winning site on Winnie the Pooh.

Mythology and Folklore

A useful site with excellent links to folklore, myth and legend electronic texts is:

Folklore, Myth and Legend

http://www.ucalgary.ca/~dkbrown/storfolk.html

Another good electronic text site for folklore and mythology is:

Folklore and Mythology Electronic Texts

`http://www.pitt.edu/~dash/folktexts.html`

Good links to mythology and folklore sites are found at:

Mythology and Folklore

`http://www.pibburns.com/mythfolk.htm`

This site is slightly fishy, but will provide you with everything you need to know about mermaids.

Mermaids

`http://www.mermaid.net/`

If you are interested in mythology in Western painting visit:

Mythology in Western Art

`http://www-lib.haifa.ac.il/www/art/`
`mythology_westart.html`

Social Studies Methods

Social Studies, because of its use of original documents (diaries, deeds, census records) and visual sources (photographs, art work, maps), is an extremely rich area on the Internet and the World Wide Web. Excellent gateway sites include:

The History Beat

`http://history.searchbeat.com`

World History Compass

`http://www.worldhistorycompass.com/index.htm`

If you want to find out what happened on a specific date visit "This Day in History":

This Day in History

`http://www.9online.com/today/today.htm`

Individual historical periods can be found at sites such as:

Civil War

http://www.homepages.dsu.edu/jankej/civilwar/
civilwar.htm

The Psychedelic '60s

http://www.lib.virginia.edu/exhibits/sixties/

General history and social studies Web sites can be linked to at:

History on PBS

http://www.pbs.org/neighborhoods/history

Public televisions guide to its historical programming for educators and others.

History/Social Studies Web Site for K–12 Teachers

http://www.execpc.com/~dboals/boals.html

Resources on the Web for teaching Social Studies and History.

Sites for Teachers

http://www.sitesforteachers.com

Lesson plans and related resources for teachers.

Genealogy is a great subject to integrate into courses in American history, as well as state and local history. Gateway sites can be found at:

Genealogy.Com

http://www.genealogy.com

Gengateway.Com

http://www.gengateway.com/

Gen Source (Genealogy Gateway)

http://www.gensource.com/ifoundit/

More practical "how to do it" sites can be found at:

Genealogy "How-To" Guide

`http://www.familytreemaker.com/mainmenu.html`

A step-by-step guide to studying genealogy.

Family Search

`http://www.familysearch.org/`

The Jesus Christ of the Latter-day Saints Web site is perhaps the best site of its type anywhere.

The Genealogy Page (National Archives)

`http://www.nara.gov/genealogy/`

The National Archives is an invaluable source of information for genealogists, providing both original records and guidelines.

Surname Origin List

`http://www.familychronicle.com/surname.html`

Find out where many surnames came from at this site.

The art and architecture of cemeteries and tombstones is a fascinating topic. It can be explored at length by visiting:

Tombstone Rubbings

`http://amberskyline.com/treasuremaps/t_stone.html`

Maps are an invaluable resource for social studies teachers at all levels of the educational system. The World Wide Web has many excellent map resources. Among the most useful are:

Click a Map

`http://www.atlapedia.com/online/map_index.htm`

Be able to select a map for any part of the world.

Earth Rise

`http://earthrise.sdsc.edu/`

A database of photographs of earth taken from space.

Geography Resources from the U.S. Census Bureau

http://www.census.gov/geo/www/

Access geographical resources from the U.S. Census Bureau.

How Far is It?

http://www.indo.com/distance/

Use the Web to measure the distance between most places in the country or the world.

Quick Maps

http://www.theodora.com/maps/abc_world_maps.html

Easily downloadable maps for all of the World.

Vintage Panoramic Maps (Library of Congress)

http://lcweb2.loc.gov/ammem/pmhtml/

Panoramic maps included in collections at the Library of Congress.

A gateway for historical documents that can be used by teachers can be found at:

Historical Documents

http://w3.one.net/~mweiler/ushda/list.htm

Examples of sites with excellent collections of historical documents include:

Documents in Law, History and Diplomacy

http://www.yale.edu/lawweb/avalon/avalon.htm

Outstanding gateway site from Yale University.

Thomas Historical Documents

http://lcweb2.loc.gov/const/constquery.html

Historical documents such as the Constitution.

Emancipation Proclamation

http://www.nara.gov/exhall/featured-document/eman/emanproc.html

An electronic text of the Civil War's most important document.

Historical Documents

http://odur.let.rug.nl/~usa/D/

An extensive collection of online documents in American and European history.

If you want to find different types of history timelines to use in your classes, then go to the following gateway site:

History Timelines

http://history.searchbeat.com

If you find yourself teaching a course that includes information on your state or local community, you will find the following state addresses helpful:

Alabama

http://www.state.al.us/2k1

Alaska

http://www.state.ak.us/

Arizona

http://www.az.gov/

Arkansas

http://www.state.ar.us/

California

http://www.ca.gov/

Colorado

http://www.state.co.us/

Connecticut

http://www.state.ct.us/

Delaware

http://delaware.gov

Research Navigator Guide: Education

Florida

http://www.state.fl.us/

Georgia

http://www.state.ga.us/

Hawaii

http://www.state.hi.us/

Idaho

http://www.accessidaho.org/index.html

Illinois

http://www.state.il.us/

Indiana

http://www.state.in.us/

Iowa

http://www.state.ia.us/

Kansas

http://www.accesskansas.org

Kentucky

http://www.kydirect.net

Louisiana

http://www.state.la.us/

Maine

http://www.state.me.us/

Maryland

http://www.mec.state.md.us/

Massachusetts

http://www.state.ma.us/

Michigan

http://www.michigan.gov

Minnesota

http://www.state.mn.us/

Mississippi

http://www.mississippi.gov

Missouri

http://www.state.mo.us/

Nebraska

http://www.state.ne.us/

Nevada

http://silver.state.nv.us/

New Hampshire

http://www.state.nh.us/

New Jersey

http://www.state.nj.us/

New Mexico

http://www.state.nm.us/

New York

http://www.state.ny.us/

North Carolina

http://www.ncgov.com

North Dakota

http://discovernd.com/

Ohio

http://www.state.oh.us/

Oklahoma

http://www.state.ok.us/

Oregon

http://www.state.or.us/

Pennsylvania

http://www.state.pa.us/

Rhode Island

http://www.info.state.ri.us/

South Carolina

http://www.myscgov.com

South Dakota

http://www.state.sd.us/

Tennessee

http://www.state.tn.us/

Texas

http://www.state.tx.us/

Utah

http://www.utah.gov

Vermont

http://www.state.vt.us/

Virginia

http://www.state.va.us/

Washington

http://access.wa.gov/

West Virginia

http://www.state.wv.us/

Wisconsin

http://www.wisconsin.gov

Wyoming

http://www.state.wy.us/

Information on world cultures can be found at the following Web addresses:

Asia Society

http://www.asiasociety.org/

Among the country's museums of Asian art and culture.

Data Base Europe

http://www.asg.physik.uni-erlangen.de/europa/
indexe.htm

A geographical database for European culture.

Latin American Network Information Center

http://lanic.utexas.edu/

Resources on all aspects of Latin America.

The World Factbook

http://www.odci.gov/cia/publications/factbook/

The Central Intelligence Agency's main online factbook.

Online sources related to Economics that could be useful in the classroom include:

Economic Statistics

http://www.cbs.nl/en/services/links/default.asp

The Netherlands online electronic database for economics.

History of Economic Thought

http://socserv2.socsci.mcmaster.ca/~econ/ugcm/3113/

An attempt to gather all material for the study of the history of economics on a single Web site.

If you want to explore inflation and the consumer price index visit:

Federal Reserve System

`http://www.federalreserve.gov/`

The main Web site for the Federal Reserve.

Consumer Price Indexes

`http://stats.bls.gov/cpi`

General information on the Consumer Price Index.

Gateway sites for archeology include:

Archeology Related Links

`http://www.arch.dcr.state.nc.us/links.htm`

Gateway site for archeology.

Arch Net

`http://archnet.asu.edu/archnet`

ArchNet serves as the World Wide Web Virtual Library for Archaeology, and provides access to a wide range of archaeological resources available on the Internet.

Examples of archeological sites that can be used to support teaching include:

Biblical Archeology

`http://www.lpl.arizona.edu/~kmeyers/archaeol/`
`bib_arch.html`

Sources on archeology and the Bible.

Classics and Mediterranean Archeology

`http://rome.classics.lsa.umich.edu/`

Gateway site to the Classics and Ancient archeology.

Egyptian Artifacts Exhibit

`http://www.memphis.edu/egypt/artifact.html`

The University of Memphis Institute of Egyptian Art and Archaeology home page

Research Navigator Guide: Education

Megalithic Portal

http://www.megalithic.co.uk

A gateway to information about Megalithic sites.

Petroglyphs and Rock Painting

http://www.execpc.com/~jcampbel/

Pertoglyphs and rock painting from the Southwest.

Resources on architecture include:

ADAM (the Art, Design, Architecture & Media Information Gateway)

http://adam.ac.uk/

A major gateway site.

The Ancient City of Athens

http://www.indiana.edu/~kglowack/athens/

An online tour of ancient Athens.

Gothic Dreams

http://www.elore.com/elore04.html

Great Gothic architecture and its history.

Frank Lloyd Wright Foundation

http://www.franklloydwright.org/

The official site for America's greatest architect.

Look into specialized subject areas to help students develop an interest in historical information. The history of aviation, for example, provides a great place to jump off into the study of history. Examples of sites you could start with include:

Airship and Blimp Resources

http://www.hotairship.com/

Resources on all aspects of airships and blimps.

The Aviation History Online Museum

http://www.aviation-history.com/

A superb online collection of photos and related sources dealing with the history of aviation.

The K–8 Aeronautics Internet Textbook

http://wings.avkids.com

The basics of aviation for kids.

National Air and Space Museum

http://www.nasm.edu/

America's great museum of flight.

Science Methods

General reference and science gateway sites of interest include:

Cornell Theory Center Math & Science Gateway

http://www.tc.cornell.edu/Edu/MathSciGateway

MathSciGateway/Explore Science

http://www.explorescience.com

Science Education Gateway

http://cse.ssl.berkeley.edu/segway/

Frank Potter's Science Gems

http://sciencegems.com/

Look up world records and learn about the extremes in science.

Extreme Science

http://www.extremescience.com/index.htm

Research Navigator Guide: Education

If you want to ask a scientist questions, visit:

MadSci Net: The Laboratory that Never Sleeps

http://www.madsci.org/

Visit the home page for television's most popular science educator.

Bill Nye The Science Guy!

http://www.billnye.com

Information on Science Fairs can be found at:

Science Fair Project Resource Guide

http://www.ipl.org/youth/projectguide/

Other useful science fair sites include:

Science Fairs Home Page

http://www.stemnet.nf.ca/~jbarron/scifair.html

A science fair site designed to help students develop an original research project.

Ultimate Science Fair Resource

http://www.scifair.org/

The ultimate science fair site with everything you need to know to create a competitive project.

Useful biology sites include:

Surf Sites for Cyber Biology

http://ucsu.colorado.edu/~marcora/surf.htm

Outstanding gateway site.

BioChem Links

http://biochemlinks.com/bclinks/bclinks.cfm

Chemistry and Biology links on the Web.

Information on science and health can be found at the following federal and international sites:

Centers for Disease Control

`http://www.cdc.gov/`

The government's main center for fighting diseases.

National Institutes of Health

`http://www.nih.gov/`

The main government research center dealing with health issues.

U.S. Department of Health and Human Services

`http://www.os.dhhs.gov/`

One of the main site for health issues in the federal government.

World Health Organization

`http://www.who.int/`

The main international health organization.

Some good gateway sites for animals include:

Birdwatching WWW Links

`http://www.interlog.com/~gallantg/birdlink.html`

Links for birdwatchers.

Bill's Wildlife Sites

`http://www.wildlifer.com/wildlifesites/`

Directory of sites for wildlife.

Zooweb

`http://www.zooweb.com/`

Links to the world's major zoos.

Specific animal Web sites include:

Birding Tips for All Seasons

http://www.birdwatching.com/birdingtips.html

Tips on birdwatching.

Cat Fanciers

http://www.fanciers.com/

A great general Web site about cats.

Canine Web

http://www.canine-connections.com/

Comprehensive information on dogs.

Electronic Zoo

http://netvet.wustl.edu/e-zoo.htm

Veterinary information on the Web.

Horse Web

http://www.horseweb.com/links/

Links to resources about horses.

Marine Mammals

http://www.mmsc.org/info/

Information about marine mammals and stranding.

House Rabbit Society

http://www.rabbit.org/

An all-volunteer, nonprofit organization that rescues rabbits and educates the public on rabbit care and behavior.

A Master Piece of Evolution—The Shark

http://www.ncf.carleton.ca/~bz050/HomePage.shark.html

General information about sharks.

Information on endangered animals can be found at:

Endangered Species

`http://endangered.fws.gov/index.html`

For sources on the environment consult:

Environmental Organization Web Directory

`http://www.webdirectory.com/`

A search engine for things environmental.

Greenpeace

`http://www.greenpeace.org/`

One of the World's leading ecological activist groups.

Population Index on the Web

`http://popindex.princeton.edu/`

Major resources for the study of population.

Geology sites can be found at:

Geology Link

`http://www.geologylink.com/`

General resources on Geology.

National Geophysical Data Center

`http://www.ngdc.noaa.gov/`

The national repository for geophysical data, providing a wide range of science data services and information

U.S. Geological Survey

`http://info.er.usgs.gov/`

The main federal government site dealing with geology and related issues.

Mathematics Methods

There is a wealth of material available on mathematics on the Web. Check out some of the following sites:

Ask Dr. Math

`http://mathforum.org/dr.math/`

Answers to classic math problems and more.

Geometry Through Art

`http://mathforum.org/~sarah/shapiro`

A site for exploring art through Mathematics.

Math Goodies

`http://www.mathgoodies.com/`

Math Goodies is a free educational Web site featuring interactive math lessons, homework help, worksheets, puzzles, message boards, and more.

Mega Math

`http://www.c3.lanl.gov/mega-math/index.html`

Los Alamos National Laboratory's site for kids and teachers in interested in Mathematics.

Space Exploration and Astronomy

An excellent gateway site for astronomy can be found at:

WebStars

`http://heasarc.gsfc.nasa.gov/docs/www_info/webstars.html`

For information on space exploration and astronomy, visit:

The Constellations and Their Stars

`http://www.astro.wisc.edu/~dolan/constellations/`

Other interesting astronomy related sites include:

Exploring Mars

`http://cass.jsc.nasa.gov/expmars/expmars.html`

This Web site provides access to a variety of educational resources about Mars that have been developed at NASA's Lunar and Planetary Institute.

Galileo Mission

`http://www.jpl.nasa.gov/galileo/`

NASA's resilient Galileo spacecraft keeps sending back data for researchers. Learn more about it and its mission at this site.

Mars Exploration

`http://mars.jpl.nasa.gov/`

General site on Mars exploration. Lots of classroom activities.

Planetary Fact Sheets

`http://nssdc.gsfc.nasa.gov/planetary/planetfact.html`

Great activities to use in the classroom can be linked to at:

NASA Kids

`http://kids.msfc.nasa.gov/`

NASA's special Web site for kids.

Library Resources for Educators on the Internet and World Wide Web

Many university and public libraries are making their catalogs available through the World Wide Web. They represent an enormously useful and convenient resource for educators. It is almost certain that your university or college will have a major library Web site and that you will be able to connect to it. In order to find the Web address for your school's library, do a general search for your university's home page. Once you get to the home page, you can usually find a menu item or link to your school's library.

You can use this approach to get to almost any major university library site in the country.

Library resources and links can be found at:

Research Navigator Guide: Education

Library WWW Servers

http://sunsite.berkeley.edu/libweb/

Other library sites that you might find interesting to explore include:

American Library Association

http://www.ala.org

The University of California at Berkeley

http://www.lib.berkeley.edu

Library of Congress Site

http://www.loc.gov

New York Public Library Home Page

http://www.nypl.org/

Portico—The British Library

http://portico.bl.uk/

University of Virginia Library

http://www.lib.virginia.edu/

University of Waterloo Library

http://www.lib.uwaterloo.ca

College and University Home Pages

http://www.mit.edu/people/cdemello/univ.html

University of California Santa Cruz Campus

http://www.ucsc.edu/library/index.html

United Kingdom Public Libraries on the Web

http://dspace.dial.pipex.com/town/square/ac940/
weblibs.html

Electronic texts can be found at many World Wide Web sites. Most are searchable, which means you can conduct interesting types of research using them. For example, suppose you decide that you want to write a paper on the use of the word death in the tragedies of Shakespeare. Going online would make it possible for you to find an electronic database where you could search for every place the word is used in his plays.

Probably the best source for electronic books is Project Gutenberg. The project currently has several hundred books available online in fully searchable format. You can find it on the World Wide Web at:

Project Gutenberg

```
http://promo.net/pg/
```

In order to search for electronic book resources online, check:

Alex—A Catalog of Electronic Texts on the Internet

```
http://sunsite.berkeley.edu/alex/
```

Other useful sources include:

The Internet Classics Archive

```
http://classics.mit.edu
```

A total of 441 classics from Ancient literature available online at this site.

The On-Line Books Page

```
http://onlinebooks.library.upenn.edu
```

Over 13,000 sources at this site can be explored.

Other valuable electronic collections include:

Bartleby Library

```
http://www.bartleby.com/
```

A major archive of electronic books.

The Electronic Text Center at the University of Virginia:

```
http://etext.lib.virginia.edu/uvaonline.html
```

One of the country's main centers for electronic books.

The On-Line Medieval and Classical Library:

```
http://sunsite.berkeley.edu/OMACL
```

Online sources in Medieval and Classical literature.

Resources on almost every specialized genre of literature can be found on the Internet and the World Wide Web. Poetry Web sites, for example, can be found at:

British Poetry 1780–1910: A Hypertext Archive

`http://etext.lib.virginia.edu/britpo.html`

Excellent archive of British poetry.

Electronic Poetry Center Home Page

`http://epc.buffalo.edu/`

Watch poetry come alive on this electrifying Web site.

Lost Poets of the Great War

`http://www.emory.edu/ENGLISH/LostPoets/index.html`

A useful site on poets of the First World War.

Science fiction Web sites include:

Linköping Science Fiction and Fantasy

`http://sf.www.lysator.liu.se/sf_archive/`

Books and film reviews and all things science fiction.

MIT Science Fiction Society Home Page

`http://www.mit.edu/activities/mitsfs/homepage.html`

Interested in researching science fiction titles online? The MIT Science Fiction Society has what is probably the largest database on science fiction books found anywhere on the Internet.

Sources on critical theory and literature include:

Cyberspace, Hypertext, and Critical Theory

`65.107.211.206/cpace/cspaceov.html`

Web resources on women writers include:

Brown Women Writers Project

`http://www.wwp.brown.edu/wwp_home.html`

Research Navigator Guide: Education

A Celebration of Women Writers

```
http://digital.library.upenn.edu/women/
```

Feminism and Women's Studies (Carnegie-Mellon English Server)

```
http://english-www.hss.cmu.edu/Feminism.html
```

Censorship issues and banned texts can be found at:

Banned Books On-Line

```
http://digital.library.upenn.edu/books/
banned-books.html
```

A good place to browse for interesting book titles is:

Book Browser

```
http://www.Polyweb.com/BookBrowser
```

If you are looking for specific book titles or authors, there are many references that you will find helpful on the Web. *Books in Print* is the standard library reference book for finding books that are currently in print. Online, there are many booklists with interesting links. Another method of finding what is currently in print is to visit the electronic bookstore Amazon Books, which has one of the largest collections of books for sale in the world.

Amazon Books

```
http://www.amazon.com/
```

Other good book sources include:

City Lights Publishers and Booksellers

```
http://www.citylights.com/
```

The Web site for perhaps the country's most famous bookstore.

Book Wire Index—Book Awards

```
http://www.bookwire.com/bookwire/otherbooks/
Book-Awards.html
```

Learn about current book awards and prizes.

Research Navigator Guide: Education

Reference Sources

Gateways for reference sources include:

DeskRef

http://www.rcls.org/deskref

Nearly 900 links to every imaginable type of reference resource.

Internet Public Library Ready Reference

http://www.ipl.org/ref/RR/

Excellent gateway site.

Electronic reference sources can be found at:

Martindale's Reference Desk

http://www-sci.lib.uci.edu/~martindale/Ref.html

A mildly eccentric personal gateway reference site with lots of interesting links.

My Virtual Reference Desk

http://www.refdesk.com/

One of the best general sources for information on the Internet.

New York Times Navigator

http://www.nytimes.com/learning/general/navigator/index.html#ref

The *New York Times* outstanding gateway site for reference sources.

Reference Shelf

http://www.unidata.ucar.edu/staff/russ/refs.html

A good set of links to general reference sources available online.

Scholes Library Electronic Reference Desk

http://scholes.alfred.edu/ref_desk/ref.html

An excellent set of links to general reference sites from Alfred University.

Study Web Reference

http://www.studyweb.com/

Lightspan's outstanding collection of study links for K–12 includes almost every imaginable topic.

THOR Virtual Reference Desk

http://thorplus.lib.purdue.edu/reference/

An excellent set of links to online reference sites available through Purdue University.

Virtual Reference Desk

http://www.vrd.org/

Go to the locator at this Web site to find almost any type of electronic reference work you could possibly want.

Yahoo Reference

http://dir.yahoo.com/reference/index.html

Interested in finding links to online dictionaries and encyclopedias? This is the place to go.

Links to Sites on Language Usage

Style resources, guides and dictionaries include:

Common Errors in English

http://www.wsu.edu/~brians/errors/errors.html

Check correct word use, as well as find sources on English grammar and usage.

Elements of Style by William Strunk

http://www.bartleby.com/141/index.html

An online and searchable version of one of the great grammar handbooks in the English language.

Garbl's Writing Center

http://www.garbl.com

Research Navigator Guide: Education

An annotated directory of Web sites focusing on creativity, the writing process, English grammar, style and usage, reference sources, words, plain language, active writing, online writing experts, word play and books on writing.

Grammar Bytes

`http://www.chompchomp.com/menu.htm`

Learn about grammar and then test what you actually know.

Grammar Handbook University of Illinois at Urbana-Champaign

`http://www.english.uiuc.edu/cws/wworkshop/`
`grammarmenu.htm`

Explanations for all aspects of grammatical use.

Guide for Writing Research Papers

`http://cctc.commnet.edu/mla.htm`

Everything you need for getting researching and writing a paper.

LOGOS Home Page

`http://www.logos.it/`

Electronic translation online.

Modern Language Association

`http://www.mla.org`

The major academic organization for research on the English language and linguistics.

OneLook Dictionaries

`http://www.onelook.com/`

Link word searches to hundreds of different dictionaries.

Online English Grammar

`http://www.edufind.com/english/grammar/index.cfm`

Links, software and other resources involving grammar.

Sources for quotes include:

Annabelle's Quotation Guide

`http://annabelle.net/`

A good site for "quotes of the week" and other special types of quotation material.

Bartlett's Quotations (1919)

`http://www.bartleby.com/100`

The great reference source for quotations.

Creative Quotations

`http://www.bemorecreative.com/home-cq.shtml`

Among the largest and most imaginative source for quotations on the Internet and World Wide Web.

Mining Co. Guide to Quotations

`http://quotations.miningco.com/`

Find quotes under a wide range of categories.

Phrase Finder

`http://www.shu.ac.uk/web-admin/phrases/go.html`

A professional writers' resource for generating ideas for headlines, advertising copy, song lyrics etc.

Quotations Page

`http://www.starlingtech.com/quotes/`

A great site for motivational quotes or quotes of a famous author.

Quotez

`http://www.quotations.co.uk`

Search for thousands of famous quotes on this site.

Museum Resources for Educators on the Internet and World Wide Web

Probably some of the richest resources to be found on the Internet and World Wide Web are the many different Web sites that have been set up by museums. You will find these sites useful not only for your future work with students, but in your own college and university studies.

ART MUSEUMS

There are many excellent general indexes and gateway sites for art museums that you can consult on the Internet. These include:

Art in Context

http://www.artincontext.com/

Art Museum Network

http://www.amn.org/

Museum Computer Network

http://www.mcn.edu/sitesonline.htm

MUSÉE

http://www.musee-online.org/

Virtual Library Museum Pages

http://vlmp.museophile.com

World Wide Art Resources

http://wwar.com/

Resources on artists exhibiting on the World Wide Web can be found at:

Art on the Net

http://www.art.net/Welcome.html

Research Navigator Guide: Education

For gallery and art resources, check:

Internet Art Resources

`http://artresources.com`

Virtually any type of art resource can be found at:

Worldwide Arts Resources

`http://wwar.com`

The Art Archive

`http://artchive.com/core.html`

A virtual museum which includes an incredibly comprehensive collection of the world's art can be found at the Web Museum in Paris:

WEBMUSEUM PARIS

`http://www.ibiblio.org/wm`

Almost every major American and European art museum has its own Web site. Use them as a resource to learn more about individual collections or artists. Here is a list of some of the most interesting museums you can connect to on the Web:

Art Institute of Chicago

`http://www.artic.edu/aic/index.html`

One of America's greatest art museums with an outstanding online site.

Banff Centre for the Arts

`http://www.banffcentre.ab.ca/`

Check of the creative electronic center at this site.

The Brooklyn Museum

`http://www.brooklynart.org/visit/`
`permanent_collections.html`

Among the country's major art museums. The Museum's collection of ancient Egyptian art is generally acknowledged to be one of the finest in the world. The museum is also known for its controversial exhibits of modern art.

Butler Institute of American Art

http://www.butlerart.com

An interesting regional art museum. Check out the exhibit of Winslow Homer's magazine engravings.

Michael C. Carlos Museum/Emory University

http://carlos.emory.edu

The Michael C. Carlos Museum includes the largest collection of ancient art in the Southeast with objects from ancient Egypt, Greece, Rome, the Near East, and the ancient Americas, as well as collections of 19th and 20th-century sub-Saharan African art and European and American works on paper from the Renaissance to the present.

The Detroit Institute of Arts

http://www.dia.org

The sixth largest art museum in the United States, with over 60,000 works of art.

Finnish National Gallery

http://www.fng.fi/

Finland's major art museum. Don't worry, there is an English as well as Finnish version of the site.

Glenbow Museum

http://www.glenbow.org/

An interesting museum site with excellent resources on Western Canadian history.

Guggenheim Museum

http://www.guggenheim.org/

The Guggenheim is actually a series of museums from around the world, including sites in New York, Bilbao, Spain, Berlin, and Venice. The Bilbao building designed by Frank O. Gehry is among the most exciting building designs of the late twentieth century.

Houston Museum of Fine Arts

http://www.mfah.org

Comprehensive collections across many different cultures and traditions.

Research Navigator Guide: Education

The Kennedy Center's ArtsEdge

`http://artsedge.kennedy-center.org/artsedge.html`

The Kennedy's Center's site for art and online learning.

Los Angeles County Museum of Art

`http://www.lacma.org/`

Art from a wide range of cultures in one of the country's leading art museums.

Lowe Art Museum (University of Miami)

`http://www.lowemuseum.org/`

An outstanding regional and university art gallery with excellent Native American, modern and Asian collections.

Metropolitan Museum of Art

`http://www.metmuseum.org`

View over 3,500 items online from one of America's greatest art museums.

Minneapolis Institute of Arts

`http://www.artsmia.org`

One of the outstanding art museums in the Midwest. Go to their site and send and electronic postcard from the museum.

Montreal Museum of Fine Arts

`http://www.mbam.qc.ca`

An interesting contemporary art museum with innovative interactive online exhibits.

Musee du Louvre

`http://www.paris.org/Musees/Louvre/`

The home of the Mona Lisa, the Winged Victory of Samothrace, Venus de Milo and even more.

The Museum of Modern Art, New York

`http://www.moma.org/`

America's greatest modern art museum.

National Museum of American Art

http://www.nmaa.si.edu

One of the best online museum sites available.

Palmer Museum of Art

http://www.psu.edu/dept/palmermuseum/

Located at Pennsylvania State University, the Palmer Museum of Art's galleries present selections from a permanent collection which comprises thirty-five centuries of painting, sculpture, ceramics, and works on paper from the United States, Europe, Asia, and South America.

University of Memphis Institute of Egyptian Art and Archaeology

http://www.memphis.edu/egypt/main.html

Important Egyptian artifacts and materials.

De Young Fine Arts Museum of San Francisco

http://www.famsf.org

Located in Golden Gate Park in San Francisco, the de Young houses collections of American art, African art, Oceanic art, textile arts, and arts of the Americas.

Whitney Museum of American Art

http://www.whitney.org

One of America's great contemporary art museums.

HISTORICAL MUSEUMS

Historical museums not only provide valuable information on specific regions and specialized topics, but often broader historical background as well. If you are interested in learning about East Coast maritime history, for example, a visit to the Chesapeake Bay Maritime Museum will prove quite useful.

Chesapeake Bay Maritime Museum

http://www.cbmm.org/

If you want to learn about a topic such as Chicago during the Progressive Era, or the great Chicago Fire, visit the Chicago Historical Society.

Chicago Historical Society

http://www.chicagohs.org

Other interesting historical museums include:

Golden Gate Railroad Museum

http://www.ggrm.org

The Golden Gate Railroad Museum is dedicated to the preservation of steam and passenger railroad equipment, and the interpretation of local railroad history.

Henry Ford Museum & Greenfield Villa

http://www.hfmgv.org/

See the Wright Brother's workshop from Dayton, Ohio, as well as other interesting artifacts of American life and culture.

Jewish Museum, New York

http://www.jewishmuseum.org/

The largest Jewish museum in the Western hemisphere deals with all aspects of Jewish life and culture.

Mariners' Museum, Newport News, Virginia

http://www.mariner.org/

Many interesting exhibits and programs—pay particular attention to the information on recent attempts to salvage the Civil War ironclad the Monitor.

Museum of American Political Life

http://www.hartford.edu/polmus/polmus1.html

The museum of American Political Life explores the history of American politics and presidential campaigns.

Mystic Seaport Museum

http://www.mysticseaport.org/welcome.html

America's greatest nautical museum. Take a tour of an actual whaling ship, and learn about the role of sailing in the development of our country.

The National Museum of American History

`http://americanhistory.si.edu/`

The Smithsonian's main museum of American history. See the flag that inspired our national anthem "The Star Spangled Banner," as well as artifacts about almost every aspect of American life.

Old Sturbridge Village Museumhttp://www.osv.org

`http://www.osv.org`

Learn about American history through one of the country's great "living museums."

SCIENCE MUSEUMS

Many different science museum sites can be found on the Web. Like art and historical museums, they are excellent sources of information on specialized topics, as well as rich resources for the development of curriculum materials. Science museum sites can also provide important opportunities for interdisciplinary inquiry.

Academy of Natural Sciences of Philadelphia

`http://www.acnatsci.org/`

Visit Dinosaur Hall and see the 45 foot long *T. rex, Giganotosaurus* with its six foot head!

Boston Museum of Science

`http://www.mos.org/`

Don't miss the virtual fish tank created for the museum by the Massachusetts Institute of Technology.

The California Academy of Sciences

`http://www.calacademy.org/`

Earth, ocean and space are the focus of this outstanding science center.

Carnegie Science Center

`http://www.csc.clpgh.org/`

A hands-on science center that also lets you learn about the sky over Mr. Rogers's Neighborhood in Pittsburgh.

Chicago Academy of Sciences Nature Museum

http://www.chias.org/

Be sure to take a look at the interactive exhibit on the environment.

Fernbank Museum of Natural History

http://www.fernbank.edu/museum/

Altanta, Georgia's premiere natural science museum.

The Florida Museum of Natural History

http://www.flmnh.ufl.edu/

Virtual exhibits include materials on Mayan culture and dinosaurs.

History of Science Museum in Florence, Italy

http://galileo.imss.firenze.it/index.html

Take a virtual tour and learn about Galileo and other Renaissance scientists.

Manchester Museum

http://museum.man.ac.uk/

Everything from archeology to numismatics at this site.

Miami Museum of Science

http://www.miamisci.org/

Learn about sharks and other mysteries of the ocean at this site.

National Museum of Science and Technology, Ottawa, Ontario, Canada

http://www.science-tech.nmstc.ca/

Excellent science resources available in both French and English.

Natural History Museum of Los Angeles County

http://www.nhm.org/

A great site with lots of interesting resources. Take a special look at the exhibit on Johann Christian Dan Schreber's 1744 multivolume set of books entitled *Die Saugthiere in Abbildungen nach der Natur mit Beschreibungen*. Focusing on mammals of the world.

The New Mexico Museum of Natural History and Science

`http://www.nmmnh-abq.mus.nm.us/nmmnh/dinosinnm.html`

Great dinosaur and fossil material, plus lots more.

North Carolina Museum of Life and Science

`http://www.ncmls.org`

Visit the butterfly house and more at the North Carolina Museum of Life and Science.

Oregon Museum of Science and Industry

`http://www.omsi.edu/`

Online activities and more available for educators.

St. Louis Science Center

`http://www.slsc.org/`

The St. Louis Science Center focuses on astronomy, space sciences and aviation, and is one of the outstanding centers for space education in the country.

Science Museum of Virginia

`http://www.smv.org/`

A good general museum site with activities for students including a simulated space lander simulator.

Science World (Vancouver, British Columbia, Canada)

`http://www.scienceworld.bc.ca/frameset.html`

An outstanding regional science center with great activities for kids.

SciTech Science and Technology Interactive Center

`http://scitech.mus.il.us`

A great Web site for getting into hands-on science.

The Smithsonian Institution, National Museum of Natural History

http://nmnhwww.si.edu

Can't go to Washington, D.C. to visit the Natural History Museum? Then take a virtual tour at this Web site.

The Swedish Museum of Natural History

http://www.nrm.se/

Resources on animals, plants, fossils, astronomy and similar types of topics.

University of Georgia Museum of Natural History

http://museum.nhm.uga.edu/

Particularly outstanding at this site is the material on Georgia wildlife.

How Schools Use the World Wide Web

Schools at all levels of the educational system are setting up their own Web sites. Nearly anything that is done administratively or educationally in a school can be incorporated into a Web site. Here are some of the types of information you will typically find at a school site:

- Background about the school, its address, key phone numbers, and so on.
- Information about the community.
- Teacher home pages including photographs, biographies, and lesson plans.
- Student home pages, including personal essays, examples of written work, drawing and photographs.
- Special academic projects: results of experiments, international exchanges, field trips, essays, poetry, fiction, artwork, and the like.
- Extracurricular activities: clubs, literary magazines, yearbook, sports schedules and results, and student government documents.
- Parent and community resources such as PTSA newsletters.
- School, community, and lunch calendars.

The best way to really get a sense of what schools are doing is to visit different sites across the country, and even around the world.

Exploring School Web Sites

Perhaps there is no better place to check the types of projects that are being done by schools using the Internet and the World Wide Web than to visit Web 66, a project sponsored by the 3-M Corporation and the University of Minnesota School of Education. Web 66 provides lists of the addresses of hundreds of schools both here and abroad:

Web66

`http://web66.coled.umn.edu/`

The goals of the Web 66 project are: 1. to help K–12 educators learn how to set up their own Internet servers; 2. to link K–12 Web servers and the educators and students at those schools; and 3. to help K–12 educators find and use K–12 appropriate resources on the Web.

For an extensive list of school Web sites at all levels of the educational system, as well as from around the world, Web 66's Internet Registry is outstanding:

WWW Schools Registry

`http://web66.coled.umn.edu/schools.html`

Probably the oldest and most complete list of school Web servers. A great place to be able to search for interesting school sites.

A useful tool for finding school Web sites from around the world is:

School Net Navigator

`http://school.net/go/navigator`

This site links to over 4,000 Web sites around the world. It allows users to designate a wide range of subject and demographic variables for each search.

Special Internet Sites Useful in Multicultural Education

General Diversity Sites

Diversity Resources

`http://www.ed.wright.edu/diversity/`

This is a comprehensive site for many resources concerning diversity issues. This mega-site contains many multicultural resources

The Equity Center

http://www.nwrel.org/cnorse/index.html

The mission of the Equity Center of the Northwest Regional Educational Laboratories is to help public school personnel embrace the key concepts of equity and eliminate bias and discrimination (overt or subtle, unconscious or intentional, personal or institutional) in their day-to-day activities

American Civil Liberties Union

http://www.aclu.org/

An electronic resource providing vast information on every topic related to diversity.

16 Elements of Effective Teacher Education for Diversity

http://www.ncrel.org/sdrs/areas/issues/educatrs/ presrvce/pe3lk5.htm

Kenneth M. Zeichner (1993) wrote Educating Teachers for Cultural Diversity (NCRTL Special Report) and included his 16 elements. This Web page accesses a thorough explanation of these 16 elements.

Teaching Young Children To Resist Bias

http://npin.org/library/pre1998/n00123/n00123.html

The early years are the time to begin helping children form strong, positive self-images and grow up to respect and get along with people who are different from themselves. If we want children to like themselves and value diversity, we must learn how to help them resist the biases and prejudices that are still far too prevalent in our society.

Center for Multilingual Multicultural Research

http://www.usc.edu/dept/education/CMMR/

The Center is an organized research unit at the University of Southern California, facilitating the research collaboration, dissemination and professional development activities of faculty, students, and others across School of Education, university and outside organizational lines.

American Forum for Global Education Newsletter

http://www.globaled.org/issues/index.html

This site deals with important issues that concern educators and education policymakers. It also talks about the way schools are dealing with these issues.

Center for Multilingual/Multicultural Research

`http://www-bcf.usc.edu/~cmmr/BEResources.html`

This site provides relevant articles, links and resources for Multilingual and Multicultural Research.

Electronic Magazine of Multicultural Education

`http://www.eastern.edu/publications/emme/`

This online E-magazine publishes writings with respect to multicultural education, which include instructional ideas, reviews of literary and multimedia resources; and scholarly articles.

National Association for Multicultural Education Washington, DC

`http://www.nameorg.org/`

This site has immense resources with respect to Multicultural Education. There are tools for aiding teachers in developing a curriculum that is multicultural.

Diversity Web, an interactive resource hub for Higher Education

`http://www.diversityweb.org/`

This site provides online discussion forums. Resources on DiversityWeb are organized around seven Campus Diversity Priorities.

Teaching Tolerance

`http://www.splcenter.org/teachingtolerance/`
`tt-index.html`

Teaching tolerance is a National Project for helping teachers foster Equity, Understanding and respect in classrooms and beyond. This site provides free or low-cost resources to educators and funding as well. It also provides a review of the latest and best multicultural education materials.

Crosspoint Anti-Racism

`http://www.magenta.nl/crosspoint`

Over 1000 different links to over a hundred countries to view topics concerning anti-racism.

Research Navigator Guide: Education

Multicultural Resources

United Nations World Wide Web Project

`http://www.valdosta.peachnet.edu/~markswif/intro.html`

Peace Education Now and a growing number of educational and service organizations are using electronic networking to create a gift of peace education in recognition of the 50th Anniversary of the United Nations.

Multicultural Education and the Internet

`http://curry.edschool.Virginia.EDU/curry/centers/`
`multicultural/net/net.html`

Contains a tool for evaluation of the Multiculturalism and the World Wide Web: commentary on the "multicultural-ness" of the World Wide Web; how to evaluate Web sites from a multicultural perspective; a checklist to evaluate education Web sites from a multicultural approach

Diversity

`http://home.earthlink.net/~dboals1/diversit.html`

Mega-site for social studies teachers and others providing electronic resources under a variety of categories related to diversity.

Adversity Net: For Victims of Preferential Treatment

`http://www.adversity.net/`

This site invitees discussion of reverse discrimination and supports fair and equal treatment under the law without regard to race, and without racial preferences. The organization opposes racial discrimination against anyone, including racial discrimination against non-minorities and provides information and assistance to victims of reverse discrimination.

Pathways to School Improvement

`http://www.ncrel.org/sdrs/pathways.htm`

Pathways is a Web site which was designed primarily to help school improvement teams as they progress through the phases of the School Improvement Cycle down a path towards meaningful engaged learning.

Teacher Talk Home Page

`http://education.indiana.edu/cas/tt/ttarticles.html`

This is a site designed especially for pre-service teachers preparing to teach in the secondary schools. It contains practical information, strategies and suggestions for those preparing to teach secondary students. Much of the information provided is related to diversity in the classroom.

African Americans in science: Books for young readers.

```
http://www.ed.gov/databases/ERIC_Digests/
ed382455.html
```

Just Us Books. (1995). What is an authentic multicultural book?

```
http://www.mpec.org/WhatIs.html
```

In Motion Magazine

```
http://www.inmotionmagazine.com
```

In Motion Magazine is a multicultural, online U.S. publication about democracy.

Age

CHILDREN-YOUTH

The American Academy of Child and Adolescent Psychiatry: Facts for Families

```
http://www.aacap.org/publications/factsfam/index.htm
```

The AACAP is a national professional medical association dedicated to treating and improving the quality of life for children, adolescents, and families affected by mental, behavioral, or developmental disorders. Links are provided which supply assistance to children and their families.

The Black Community's Crusade for Children

```
http://www.childrensdefense.org/bccc.htm
```

Coordinated nationally by the Children's Defense Fund, the BCCC seeks to: enrich the lives of black children through involvement of the black community, younger and older, involve black leaders in the future success of the young, and to "identify, train, nurture, link, and empower a new generation of effective Black servant-leaders younger than 30."

Children's Defense Fund (CDF)

```
http://www.childrensdefense.org/
```

The posted mission of CDF is to "Leave No Child Behind" and to "ensure every child a Healthy Start, a Head Start, a Fair Start, a Safe Start, and a

Research Navigator Guide: Education

Moral Start in life and successful passage to adulthood with the help of caring families and communities." Links available to help children get that start in life.

Children's Rights Council (CRC)

http://www.gocrc.com/

The CRC is a national organization whose mission is to assure children meaningful and continuing contact with both of their parents and extended family regardless of the parents' marital status.

Child Rights Information Network

http://www.crin.org/

CRIN is a global network of organizations sharing their experiences of information on children's rights. Their site offers quick access to important documentation and information on selected topics related to children's rights around the world.

The Future of Children

http://www.futureofchildren.org/

Links to journal articles written on major issues related to children's well-being, such as children's health issues, child abuse and neglect, providing adequate and appropriate child care and education, etc.

The UNICEF International Child Development Centre

http://www.unicef-icdc.org/

UNICEF has a compelling mandate—"to act as an advocate for the protection of children's rights; to help meet their basic needs; and to expand their opportunities to reach their full potential." The UNICEF International Child Development Centre (ICDC) in Florence, Italy, is an international knowledge base and training centre focusing on the rights of children.

Arizona's Child Abuse Infocenter

http://www.ahsc.arizona.edu/ACAInfo/

The InfoCenter acts as a clearinghouse for information, consultations, and training opportunities for professionals dealing with child abuse issues throughout Arizona including the unique issues of children with disabilities and special health care needs.

Voices of Youth

http://www.unicef.org/voy/

This Web site focuses on discrimination against children in many forms.

TEENS/YOUNG ADULTS (GENERATION X)

Americans for a Society Free From Age Restrictions (ASFAR)

http://www.asfar.org/

ASFAR is an organization that is dedicated to protecting and advancing the legal civil rights of youth. ASFAR fights the voting age, curfew laws, and other laws that limit the freedom of young people.

Association for Children's Suffrage (ACS)

http://www.brown.edu/Students/
Association_for_Childrens_Suffrage/

A student organization that's challenge the voting age through lobbying, public meeting, and media. It contains support documentation for this effort as well as ideas and activities related to the topic.

Discrimination Against Youth

http://members.tripod.com/~DaysEnd/index.html

There are rising levels of discrimination against youth, in attitudes, in housing, in public businesses. Resources related to this type of discrimination are presented.

Teen Focus

http://webhome.idirect.com/~mccann/index.html

Useful information on common teenage issues can be obtained at this site. It includes writings on teens by teens

The Open Door

http://www.mcs.bc.ca/od_index.htm

Many youth feel discriminated against due to their age in places where they visit, shop, seek health care, and recreate. This site explores this topic and adds links to similar resources.

Youthwork Links and Ideas

http://www.youthwork.com/

A site for people who work with youth and for youth themselves.

Youth in Action Network

http://www.teaching.com/act/

Youth in Action Network is an interactive online service for youth, educators, organization members and classrooms who want to learn about, and participate in, positive social action and service projects

OLDER ADULT

Ageism

http://www.un.org/esa/socdev/ageing/index.html

The mission of this Web site is to "contribute to the creation of an international community that offers opportunities and higher standards of living for people of all ages." This site offers information and policy considerations on ageism.

Elder Abuse and Neglect

http://www.urbanext.uiuc.edu/elderabuse/index.html

Contains definitions and warning signs of elder abuse and neglect including physical, sexual, emotional abuse, neglect and financial exploitation

Elder Web

http://www.elderweb.com/

This is a comprehensive mega-site for on eldercare issues ElderWeb is an online sourcebook with multiple reviewed links to information about health, financing, housing, aging, and other issues related to the care of the elderly.

Gray Panthers

http://www.graypanthers.org

The mission of the Gray Panthers is to advocate and educate for social change by addressing issues such as national health care, job, social security, housing, sustainable environment, education, and peace.

International Year of Older Persons

http://www.un.org/esa/socdev/iyop/index.html

The year 1999 is the International Year of the Older Person. This site links to information, events and issues regarding the older person internationally.

TEACHING RESOURCES

The Foundation for Grandparenting

http://grandparenting.org/

The Foundation For Grandparenting is dedicated to raising "grandparent Consciousness" and "grandparent identity". Through education, research, programs, communication, and networking, they promote the involvement of grandparents as agents of positive change for families and society.

Grandparents Raising Grandchildren

http://www.uwex.edu/ces/gprg/gprg.html

Includes information on an issue that is becoming more and more widespread, i.e. grandparents raising their grandchildren.

TECA: Parents' Toolbox

http://www.fastlane.net/~eca/parentstoolbox.html

This page has information for parents regarding their child's education.

National Institute on Aging: What is your Aging IQ?

http://iucar.iu.edu/geninfo.php3

A questionnaire to reflect the reader's attitudes about aging—to differentiate fact from stereotype.

Intercultural Activities

http://www.mhhe.com/socscience/education/multi/activities.html

This site has activities for multicultural education courses and workshops for pre-service and in-service teachers.

Research Navigator Guide: Education

Belief Systems/Religion

RELIGIOUS PLURALISM

Finding Common Ground

http://www.freedomforum.org/templates/
document.asp?documentID=3979

Finding Common Ground is a Web site that the authors suggest will be "most useful to those school leaders and parents who understand the vital importance of achieving new solutions to old debates about religion and public education". The site provides rationale, resources and guidelines for including the discussion of religion in public school classrooms, particularly in U.S. and World History Classes. It also includes commentary on religious holidays in public schools, when and how they should be discussed; it raises the topic of singing sacred music and the use of religious symbols in the classroom.

free! The Freedom Forum Online

http://www.freedomforum.org

This site is an interactive daily newsletter that discusses issues related to freedom of religion and other first amendment rights.

The Case Against School Prayer

http://www.ffrf.org/issues/pray.html

This brochure was produced by the Freedom From Religion Foundation. In order to combat the growing influence of the Religious Right, this brochure is being mailed to schools, school districts and state Secretaries of Education across the country.

World Religion Resources

http://aril.org/World.html

Among the best resources concerning world religion on the Internet and growing diversity of the U.S. can be found at this site, with a special view to its new immigrant religious.

A Parent's Guide to Religion in the Public Schools

http://www.fac.org/publications/first/
religioninpublicschools/parentsguidereligion.pdf

Information provided by "Finding Common Ground" for parents which discusses Religious Liberty and Public Schools, Student Religious Expression including Student Prayer and Baccalaureate Services. It contains guidelines on Teaching about Religion and the celebration of Religious Holidays in the public school, and more.

Rationale and Guidelines for Teaching about Religion

```
http://www.freedomforum.org/templates/
document.asp?documentID=3979
```

The National Council for the Social Studies (NCSS) states that knowledge about religion is a characteristic of an educated person. They maintain that it is absolutely necessary for understanding and living in a world of diversity. NCSS provides guidelines and suggestion for how this study can take place in the public school system.

Religion in the Curriculum

```
http://www.freedomforum.org/templates/
document.asp?documentID=3979
```

This site describes and justifies using religion in the curriculum of primary grades. In the primary/elementary levels natural opportunities arise in discussions of families and community life and instruction of festivals and different cultures. The entire report describes laws, rationales, and resources.

GENERAL RESOURCES

Finding God in Cyberspace: A Guide to Religious Studies Resources on the Internet

```
http://www.fontbonne.edu/libserv/fgic/contents.htm
```

This mega-site contains internet tools for finding religious studies teaching resources in the form of print and digital resources as well as human resources. Also is included a gateway to subject resources organized by academic disciplines and to subject resources organized by religious traditions.

Mysticism in World Religions

```
http://www.digiserve.com/mystic/
```

Multiple links are provided to information about: Jewish and Christian Mysticism as well as Islamic Mysticism (also known as Sufism), Buddhist, Hindu and Taoist Mysticism

Ontario Consultants on Religious Tolerance

```
http://www.religioustolerance.org/welcome.htm#new
```

Provides access to information on Christian and non-Christian religions. The authors make every attempt to accurate in their descriptions of both conservative, liberal, and other belief systems and inclusive, describing all sides of each issue presented.

Spirituality and Consciousness

`http://www.spiritweb.org/`

This is a WWW virtual library of information religion. Timeless questions are considered, such as: "What is religion?, "What is Spirituality?", "What is truth?". Many spiritual links are supplied by the authors.

World Religions

`http://www.socialstudies.com/c/Pages/worldreligions.html`

Provides ordering information and hypertext links to general electronic resources on world religions and additional rescues on specific belief systems such as: Buddhism, Christianity, Confucianism and the Tao, Hinduism, Jainism, and Sikhism, Islam and Sufism and Judaism.

Non-Christian Faith Groups and Ethical Systems

`http://www.religioustolerance.org/var_rel.htm`

Link to a mega-site that provides resources on non-Christian faith groups and ethical systems

Links and Topics for the Academic Study of Religion

`http://www.csuchico.edu/rs/links.html`

Links for various religions and belief systems appropriate for students of different ages

NON-CHRISTIAN RELIGIONS/BELIEF SYSTEMS

Buddhism—The Buddha's Message to Mankind

`http://home.sol.no/~kmeyer/budd1.htm`

This Web site explains the philosophy/religion of Buddhism. The authors states that it is the most tolerant of all belief systems and can co-exist with any other.

Buddhism Contents

http://www.wsu.edu/~dee/BUDDHISM/CONTENTS.HTM

This site serves as a clearinghouse for links and information about Buddhist traditions, both academic and religious. Information such as an overview of the essential concepts of Buddhism and Buddhist Scriptures are linked to the Web page.

Hinduism's Electronic Ashram

http://www.himalayanacademy.com/basics/nineq/index.html

This site answers the nine most asked questions regarding Hinduism. For example, the definition of "God", reincarnation, Karma, vegetarianism, and the meaning of the dot that many Hindu men and women wear on their foreheads.

Hindu Resources Online

http://www.hindu.org/

Mega-link to Hindu teachers and organizations, news events, locations and connections to temples and ashrams, dharma and philosophy, art, music, culture, the sciences and more.

Sufism, Sufis, Sufi Orders: Sufism's Many Paths

http://www.arches.uga.edu/~godlas/Sufism.html

Generally, Sufism is understood to be the inner, mystical, or psycho-spiritual dimension of Islam. Many Muslims believe that they are on the pathway to God and will arrive at a proximity to God after, Sufis, however, believe that it is possible to experiences a closeness to God while one is still alive.

Taoism Information Page

http://www.clas.ufl.edu/users/gthursby/taoism/

This resource page houses links to information on Taoism or Daoism, including the history, the practice, the relationship between Taoism and the martial arts and Tai Chi, and links to book and bibliographies on the religion. Information on Buddhism and Confucianism is also provided.

Jewish Studies Videotapes

http://www.lib.berkeley.edu/MRC/JewishVid.html

Department of Jewish Studies at the University of Berkeley.

Research Navigator Guide: Education

CHRISTIAN RELIGIONS/BELIEF SYSTEMS

Christian Faith Groups

http://www.religioustolerance.org/christ.htm

Link to a mega-site that provides resources on Christian faith groups and ethical systems.

Christian Mysticism

http://www.digiserve.com/mystic/external_links/
Christian/index.html

Links to information on Mysticism, Asceticism, and Monasticism within a Christian context are provided.

MISCELLANEOUS

Fellowship of the Earth

http://www.fote.org/religion/religion.htm

This site provides information and contacts pertinent to the understanding of the many and various Earth Religions, such as Paganism, Druidism, Buddhism, Patheism, Shamanism, Kabbalah and Wicca/Witchcraft, etc. The vision of this organization is one of spiritual growth within ourselves as individuals as well as a oneness with our community.

Under Shekhina's Wings

http://www.geocities.com/Athens/1501/shekfil.html

The focus of Under Shekhina's Wings is on cross-cultural and interfaith women's spirituality or feminist spirituality and religion. It is somewhat feminist in nature and includes information on Jewish, Christian and Moslem feminist beliefs, Earth Religions or Pagan feminist, and Freedom of Religion, with additional links to Bahai and mythology sources.

Native American Spirituality

http://www.religioustolerance.org/nataspir.htm

The contributions that Native American Spirituality has made on North America are described. Focus on Native Religious Development, particularly that of the Inuit peoples and the Eastern Subarctic, Eastern Woodlands, Plains and Southwest Cultures. Links to Native American resources are provided.

Class

American Social Indicators

http://www.eskimo.com/~esmik/index.html

This site offers current social class research to the student. Primary areas for discussion include indicators, questions, and discussion. The section on indicators is a nice example of hypertext and a statistical review of social class.

Bibliography on Class

http://www.pscw.uva.nl/sociosite/CLASS/bibA.html

Albert Benschop of the Department of Sociology at the University of Amsterdam has compiled a very extensive bibliography on social class. None of the entries are in hypertext.

Critical Issue: Realizing New Learning for All Students through Professional Development

http://www.ncrel.org/sdrs/areas/issues/educatrs/
profdevl/pd200.htm

Educators are increasingly realizing the impact of community involvement in teaching and learning. Culture assumes various definitions in the educational literature. This site is an important resource for assisting educators to communicate with adults of several social classes in the reform of public education.

Disney's Celebration

http://www.sjsu.edu/faculty/wooda/celebration.html

One of the newest innovations of Disney is the construction of Celebration, a planned community near Orlando. This Web site will provide some connection with other sites on the subject of social class. Included in the site are some online essays on the development and construction of Celebration and a very nice photo gallery.

Homeless in America

http://www.qvctc.commnet.edu/student/GaryOKeefe/
homeless/frame.html

A serious overview of homelessness. This page discusses the new poverty, homelessness, families, veterans, joblessness, chemical dependency, mental illness, domestic violence, health, and education.

Research Navigator Guide: Education

"The Plain People"

http://www.800padutch.com/amish.html

The Amish are a religious group who live in 22 U.S. states and in Ontario, Canada. This is an excellent page on the culture of the Amish, the Mennonites, the Brethren, and the other "Plain People" which contains some very good photos and is very descriptive of the "plain people." This page may reflect a different dimension of discussions on social class

Social Class in Contemporary Societies

http://www.spc.uchicago.edu/SocialClass/about.html

Social Class in contemporary societies is an electronic medium for scholars to discuss social class. An article index (hypertext) is provided, and a relevant set of links are also provided.

Social Class and Poverty

http://www.abacon.com/sociology/soclinks/sclass.html

This is an Allyn and Bacon commercial site. This page has numerous links, and is categorized as follows: general sites on social class and poverty, the homeless, and hunger.

Social Class and Stratification

http://www.mtsu.edu/~baustin/COURSES/SOC401/401syll.html

Sociology 401/501—This page is a syllabus for a class on social class and stratification. This syllabus is a good introduction to these two concepts.

Welfare Mom Home Page

http://www.geocities.com/CapitolHill/1064/

A welfare mother discusses some of the myth of welfare. Readings, resources and links are provided. Of particular value is the self portrait written by the author.

The Underclass and the Culture of Poverty

http://www.maxwell.syr.edu/maxpages/classes/ECN258/undercla.htm

This site provides for a discussion of both concepts, underclass and culture of poverty. These concepts are reviewed from several sociological perspectives.

WWW Virtual Library: Sociology

http://www.mcmaster.ca/socscidocs/w3virtsoclib/
socnet.htm

This is a very serious Web site for the study of social class as well as many other issues in sociology. This is truly a megasite for students of sociology.

Exceptionalities

GENERAL

People First Language

http://www.kidstogether.org/pep-1st.htm

This Web site promulgates the use of people first language when describing children and adults with disabilities. Since our language reflects our values, our language must change. Change in language will assist in achievement of the goal for all Americans: to attain dignity, respect, and the opportunity to participate fully in American life.

The Federal Resource Center for Special Education (FRC)—The Individuals with Disabilities Education Act (IDEA)

http://www.dssc.org/frc/idea.htm

FRC is a nationwide special education technical assistance network that provides a national perspective for establishing technical assistance activities across regions. The Individuals with Disabilities Education Act (IDEA) is the law that guarantees all children with disabilities access to a free and appropriate public education. This section contains links to relevant resources.

The National Information Center for Children and Youth with Disabilities (NICHCY)

http://www.NICHCY.org/

This site has merited several awards, most recently, as one of the top ten sites in terms of gender equity and education by the Women's Educational Equity Act (WEEA). It contains access to information for families, educators and community members and organizations on children with special needs, in both English and Spanish. Additionally, the NICHCY site provides personal responses to specific questions by phone or e-mail; access to many kinds of publications; and can put users in touch with other organizations and sources of help.

Special Education Resources on the Internet (SERI)

http://seriweb.com

This mega-site provides interconnections to general information on disabilities as well as on specific disabilities. Resources are provided to location legal information, associations and national professional, support, advocacy and discussion groups, as well as products and services. Informative resources for parents & educators and assistance in inclusion and transition are also provided.

Family Village—Specific Diagnosis Card Catalog

http://www.familyvillage.wisc.edu/specific.htm

Links to information on hundreds of common and very uncommon disabilities, including diagnosis, organizations, associations, advocacy groups, chatrooms, interventions, etc.

National Early Childhood Technical Assistance System (NEC*TAS)

http://www.nectas.unc.edu/

The NEC*TAS site provides information on responsive technical assistance (TA) to the programs for infants, toddlers and preschoolers with disabilities and their families. This Web page Links to an overview of the Individuals with Disabilities Education Act (IDEA) and a list of other resources on the World Wide Web related to providing services to young children with disabilities and their families.

Zero to Three: National Center for Infants, Toddlers and their Families

http://www.zerotothree.org/

A resource site for parents and professionals focusing on the needs of the "whole baby"—in context of the family and community. The organization promotes discovery and the application of new knowledge for professionals and makes the information available to family members and other caregivers.

Categories Defined by the Individuals with Disabilities Education Act (IDEA)

AUTISM

Asperger's Syndrome

http://www.autism.org/asperger.html

This article looks at Asperger's Syndrome in three ways: language, cognition, and behavior. Characteristics are listed under each of the three areas. Asperger's Syndrome is more than likely hereditary, and at this time there is no prescribed treatment for those with Asperger's Syndrome. In adulthood, many lead productive lives.

Autism Research Institute

http://www.autism.org/pdd.html

This Web site discusses PDD which is a disorder that is often associated with autism. Bernard Rimland, PhD., who authors the article wants to eliminate the label of PDD in children because he says it limits the programs that these children are enrolled in. Most of the Web page discusses reasons for eliminating the label.

Center for the Study of Autism

http://www.autism.org/contents.html

This Web site provides an overview of Autism in several different languages, as well as an explanation of the subgroups of autism and disorders thought to be related. Links are provided for information on related issues, interventions, and supportive information for siblings. Interviews and articles by researchers in the field are accessible.

Hanen Centre

http://www.hanen.org/

Introduces the Hanen program of language intervention which trains groups of parents on methods to promote the communication of their language delayed children (those with autism or PDD, Down Syndrome, Hearing Impairment, Cerebral Palsy, Global Developmental Delays and Specific Language Impairment.

Option Institute: Worldwide Teaching Center for the Option Process

http://www.Son-Rise.org/

The Option Institute The Son-Rise Program: Alternative philosophy and intervention for Families and Professionals who work with children with autism, and other pervasive developmental disorders.

Overview of Autism

http://www.autism.org/overview.html

Research Navigator Guide: Education

This Web site provides an overview of Autism, as well as an explanation of the subgroups of autism and disorders thought to be related. Information on related issues and interventions are provided.

DEAF-BLINDNESS/DEAFNESS AND HEARING IMPAIRMENTS

D-B Link: The National Information Clearinghouse on Children Who Are Deaf-Blind

http://www.tr.wosc.osshe.edu/dblink/

DB-LINK is an information and referral service that identifies, coordinates, and disseminates information related to children and youth who have deaf-blindness. It provides specific information to parents and families on: Early intervention through post-secondary school and transition between levels, and suggests models for inclusion to provide social and communication support. References to information on other important issues are provided.

Central Institute for the Deaf (CID)

http://www.cid.wustl.edu/

CID is a network of resources central to knowledge and the progressive treatment of adult and childhood deafness.

Hearing Impairment FAQs

http://www.marky.com/hearing/

The author shares suggestions for a hearing person to keep in mind when communicating with a person with a hearing impairment. Author will also answer questions online and post Q & A to his Web site

Deaf Education Web Site

http://www.deafed.net/

The goal of this Web site is to facilitate informational sharing and collaborative activities within the field of Deaf Education. Access to Web-based curricular and instructional resources for educators of the Deaf is provided.

National Association of the Deaf (NAD)

http://www.nad.org/YLC/links.html

NAD is a professional association for those involved in education, medical and technical support. This page provides links so that the reader may get in touch with state and local organizations that may supply support in the education of the child with deafness.

The National Technical Assistance Consortium (NTAC)

http://www.tr.wou.edu/ntac/

NTAC provides information and assistance for Children and Young Adults Who have Deaf-Blindness. It assists states in improving the quality of services for these individuals to increase the numbers of children, young adults, their families, and their service providers who will benefit from these services.

VISUAL IMPAIRMENTS

American Council of the Blind (ACB)

http://www.acb.org/

ACB strives to improve the well-being of people who are have blindness or visual impairments. It seeks to elevate the social, economic and cultural levels, and improve educational and rehabilitation facilities and opportunities for those with a major degree of visual impairment.

The Audio Description Home Page

http://www.nyfa.org/nyfa/artswire/spiderschool/
1997/glossary/home.html

Audio Description involves the accessibility of the visual images of theater, media, and museum exhibitions for people who have visual impairments. It has been found to be not only a significant technique for making the arts more accessible for an important but underserved population.

National Federation of the Blind

http://www.nfb.org

NFB is a consumer and advocacy organization whose purpose is to help people who are visually handicapped achieve self-confidence and self-respect. Access to information about technology available to those with visual handicaps is found at: **http://www.nfb.org/tech.htm**

MENTAL RETARDATION/DEVELOPMENTAL HANDICAPS

The Arc of the United States

http://www.thearc.org/

The Mission of Arc is to improve the quality of life for children and adults with mental retardation and their families through education, research and advocacy. This Web page provides links to help accomplish their mission, such as information on Legal and Community Services and Support, medical information, such as conditions that might be related to or contribute to mental retardation and suggestions for educators in teaching children with mental retardation.

Family Village

`http://www.familyvillage.wisc.edu/`

The Family Village is a global community that integrates electronic information, resources, and communication opportunities for persons with mental retardation and other disabilities, for their families, and for service providers.

Siblings: Brothers and Sisters of People Who Have Mental Retardation

`http://www.thearc.org/faqs/qa-siblings.html`

Information on feelings, misunderstandings, difficulties that may be experienced by people who have siblings with disabilities and what might be done to assist them.

Down Syndrome: Understanding the Gift of Life

`http://www.nas.com/downsyn/`

The Down Syndrome Web page is compiled from the contributions of members of the Down Syndrome Listserv and others. It contain national and international links to legal, advocative and educational resources.

National Association for Down Syndrome

`http://www.nads.org/`

Parental and family advocacy group which provides information and support on the topic of Down Syndrome. It is their goal to create a better environment and bring about understanding and acceptance of people with Down syndrome

OTHER IMPAIRMENTS

The American Physical Therapy Association (APTA)

`http://www.apta.org/`

APTA's goal is to foster advancement in physical therapy practice, research, and education.

United Cerebral Palsy (UCP)

http://www.ucpa.org

The Mission of UCP is to advance the independence, productivity and full citizenship of people with cerebral palsy and other disabilities. This site provides information on UCP programs and services, but also offers information links to a wide variety of disability topics.

Traumatic Brain Injury Page

http://www.neuroskills.com/index.html?main=tbi/injury.html

Traumatic brain injury normally happens when as a result of an accident, the brain ricochets inside the skull during impact. This Web site provides general information on TBI, terminology, possible interventions, health and legal issues, etc.

Federal Resources

http://www.dssc.org/frc/federal.htm#agencies

Included here are links to several Federal agencies that administer programs that affect the lives of children and adults with disabilities.

SERIOUS EMOTIONAL DISTURBANCE

Mental Help Net

http://mentalhelp.net

This site houses an award-winning, definitive online guide to mental health, psychology, and psychiatry resources. Information about mental health issues is readily accessible and understandable for educators and families.

Internet Mental Health

http://www.mentalhealth.com/

This site houses a free encyclopedia of mental health information. It contains definitions of various Mental Disorders, Treatments, Research, information on Psychiatric Medications and internet links to other sites on mental health related issues.

Anorexia: Information and Guidance for Friends and Family

http://www.mindspring.com/~cwildes

This site, written by a young girl whose sister had anorexia, provides links to newsgroups, mailing lists, chatrooms, and online help for people with suspected eating disorders and those who love them. It focuses on females, but also contains links to eating disorders in Males, Older Victims, Children, Athletes and those with Diabetics

SPECIFIC LEARNING DISABILITIES

Learning Disabilities Association of America (LDA)

http://www.ldanatl.org/

The purpose of LDA is to enhance the quality of life by advancing the education and general welfare of children and adults who manifest disabilities of a perceptual, conceptual, or coordinative nature. Links to LD resources are provided.

Learning Disabled

http://www.ehhs.cmich.edu/~mnesset/ld.html

Specific Learning Disability (S.L.D.) means a disorder in 1 or more of the basic psychological processes involved in understanding or in using language, spoken or written, which may manifest itself in an imperfect ability to listen, think, speak, read, write, spell, or to do mathematical calculations. The term includes such conditions as perceptual handicaps, brain injury, minimal brain dysfunction, dyslexia, and developmental aphasia.

SPEECH AND LANGUAGE IMPAIRMENTS

Childhood Speech Impairments

http://www.cchs.usyd.edu.au/csd//clinic/
types_of_probs.htm

This article looks at the work of the Communication Disorders treatment and Research Clinic at the University of Sydney. Their clients are children of all ages whose language ability is not to the level that would be expected for their age, cognitive ability, and level of language exposure. Most children have difficulty understanding spoken language or expressing their ideas, or both. Areas in which problems may occur are listed as well as behaviors to look for that may indicate a language problem.

The Child Who Stutters-Parents Guide

http://www.mankato.msus.edu/dept/comdis/
kuster/Parents/childwhostutters.html

This article is not only for parents, but for educators as well. Information on the background of stuttering is given, facts and causes of stuttering are listed, examples of situations which promote dysfluency are given, as well as a list of suggestions to help parents and caregivers manage a child's stuttering.

Communicating with Signs, Sounds, and Symbols

http://www.islandnet.com/osprey/donov.html

This article presents information about Augmentative and Alternative Communication. These are methods that help individuals with communication difficulties communicate more easily and effectively. The range of people who can benefit from AAC is extensive and it can benefit people of all ages in many different communication settings.

Haskins Laboratories: Language, Linguistics, Speech

http://www.haskins.yale.edu/Haskins/MISC/DEST/language.html

A mega-site providing electronic language, linguistic, and speech resources.

Problems Faced by Children with Language Disorders in the Classroom

http://www.cchs.usyd.edu.au/csd/clinic/special_clinic_programs.htm#Speech%20Pathology%20in%20Schools

This article looks at why children with language disorders often do not cope with the requirements of the normal classroom. Children with language disorders have difficulty in reading and writing. However, Speech Pathologists can assist the teacher and student with strategies for academic and social development

Silence Isn't Always Golden

http://www.nidcd.nih.gov/health/pubs_hb/silence.htm

This article focuses on how a parent or caregiver can decide if their child's hearing needs to be tested. A hearing checklist is provided for birth to 3 months, 3 to 6 months, 6 to 10 months, 10 to 15 months, 15 to 18 months, 18 to 24 months, and 24 to 36 months.

Speech on the Web

http://students.washington.edu/~liumei/assoc.html

This page is a speech synthesis jumpstation. It contains links to World Wide Web pages related to speech synthesis.

The Stuttering Home Page

http://www.mankato.msus.edu/dept/comdis/
kuster/stutter.html

Information about Stuttering, nationally and internationally, Stuttering in the popular media, stuttering vs. cluttering and other related fluency disorders, Research on Stuttering and Therapy for Stuttering.

Stuttering Prevention

http://www.prevent-stuttering.com/

Warning Signs for the Development of Early Childhood Stuttering. Lists the early warning signs of stuttering. This site includes many articles about the disorder, stuttering.

OTHER DISABILITIES/EXCEPTIONALITIES (NOT LISTED IN IDEA)

ADD/ADHD Taking Control through Knowledge

http://www.adhdnews.com/

ADDed Attractions is a supportive Web site offering assistance to educators and families of those with ADD/ADHD

Attention Deficit Disorders

http://www.angelfire.com/biz2/makemoneynet/links.html

Links to information to help provide insight, courage, imagination and patience that is needed when dealing with children diagnosed with ADHD/ODD/OCD/LD.

Born to Explore: The Other Side of ADD

http://borntoexplore.org/

Welcome to a site devoted entirely to exploring positive and alternative views of attention deficit disorder. There is a high correlation between high energy, intuitiveness, creativity, and enthusiasm, but these qualities are not viewed as positive when we diagnose the behavior as ADD or ADHD.

Children and Adults with Attention Deficit Hyperactivity Disorder (CH.A.D.D.)

http://www.chadd.org

Organization which provides information for children and adults with ADD/ADHD and their families, teachers, co-workers, friends.

Instant Access Treasure Chest

`http://128.172.170.24/ld/ld.html#ADD`

Instant access to symptoms, definitions, information on medication, and other intervention strategies.

National Attention Deficit Disorder Association

`http://www.add.org/index.html`

ADDA's mission is to provide information for people with ADD through education, research, and public advocacy. It focuses on those with ADD and their families, as well as those who interact with those who have ADD or ADHD. ADDA is especially focused on young adults and adults with ADD.

One ADD Place

`http://www.oneaddplace.com`

Links to Newsletters, Papers & Articles, References, Frequently Asked Questions, conferences, seminars, classes and meetings on ADD and ADHD. Resources such as Books, Tapes, and other Products, Professional ADD/LD services for learning, managing and support including Education, Professional Organizers, Seminars, Workshops.

Cleftline

`http://www.cleftline.org`

A site for families of those with cleft lip, cleft palate and craniofacial deformities. The American Cleft Palate-Craniofacial Association and the Cleft Palate Foundation are dedicated to improve the lives of these children in our country and around the world.

WideSmiles

`http://www.widesmiles.org/`

Provides resources for those who work and love children with cleft lip and palate difficulties.

Epilepsy Foundation of America

`http://www.efa.org/`

The Epilepsy Foundation of America is dedicated to the welfare of people with epilepsy through research, education, advocacy and service. Links to

Research Navigator Guide: Education

research, information and education and a support group for children are supplied.

Classroom Tips for Children with Sensory Integration Disorders

```
http://www.sinetwork.org/Articles/Classroom%20tips/
classroom_tips_for_children_with.htm
```

This site gives helpful general classroom organizational strategies, as well as tips for children who are oversensitive to light touch input and children who need sensory input to stay on task.

FAQs on Sensory Integration

```
http://home.earthlink.net/~sensoryint/faq.html
```

This site answers 5 questions that are frequently asked about sensory integrative dysfunction.

Marie's SI Activity List

```
http://www.mindspring.com/~mariep/si/
activities/play.html
```

This site gives activities for the following areas of concern: tactile defensiveness, vestibular, deep pressure, oral defensiveness, and fine motor.

The Relationship of Learning Problems and Classroom Performance to Sensory Integration

```
http://www.nmark.com/si/
```

This site gives a list of behaviors that may be a sign of sensory integrative dysfunction.

Definitions

```
http://www.isl.net/~cuedspmn/definiti.html
```

This site informs about Cued Speech—Cued Speech is a visual communication system designed for use with and among hearing-impaired people. In English it utilizes eight handshapes, placed in four different locations near the face.

Sensory Integration Dysfunction

```
http://www.geocities.com/Heartland/Village/
9021/sid.html
```

This site gives behaviors that may be signs that the nervous system is not functioning correctly and signs that the child can not determine where their body is in space.

SI Toys

http://www.mindspring.com/~mariep/si/
activities/toys.html

This site gives a very short list of common toys that can be used to help integrate the senses.

Signs of Sensory Integration Difficulties

http://www.geocities.com/Heartland/2085/SYMPTOMS.htm

This site describes 7 signs of sensory integration which include: hypersensitivity to touch, movement, smells, sights or sounds, hypo-reactive to sensory stimulation, activity level that is unusually high or low, coordination problems, delays in speech, language, motor skills, or academic achievement, poor organization and poor self concept.

INCLUSION/INTEGRATION

Addressing Student Behavior Problems: An IEP Team's Introduction to Functional Behavioral Assessment and Behavior Intervention Plans

http://cecp.air.org/fba/problembehavior/main.htm

The Center for Effective Collaboration and Practice (CECP) has as its goal to improve services to children and youth with emotional and behavioral disorders, by providing education, and support needed by educators and parents.

Manual on Inclusion in Public Schools

http://www.blarg.net/~building/spneeds_meshintro.html

This site tells of the movement to accept all students, including those with severe developmental disabilities, in general education programs.

Family Village—Siblings of Persons with Disabilities

http://www.familyvillage.wisc.edu/general/
frc_sibl.htm

Resources for siblings of children with disabilities.

Famous People with Disabilities

http://www.familyvillage.Wisc.Edu/general/famous.html

List of famous celebrities (sports, political, entertainment, scientists, etc.) who had specific disabilities. Ideal for use as role models for all children.

Friends of Inclusion Resource Page

http://www.inclusion.com/N-friends.of.Inclusion.html

Inclusion Press is a small independent press striving to produce readable, accessible, user-friendly books and resources about full inclusion in school, work, and community. Although this is a commercial site, they do provide access to information of great value to those who love and work with persons with special needs.

Inclusive Education

http://www.beachcenter.org/

This page from The Beach Center on Families and Disabilities is an excellent resource for teachers and parents. Provides information, supportive strategies for providing successful integration into a supported inclusion classroom.

Inclusive Education: Legal Requirements/Court Cases

http://www.uni.edu/coe/inclusion/legal/index.html

When disagreements between school districts and parents arise for the free and appropriate public education of children, solutions are often found through mediation. However, if not, an impartial hearing officer listens to testimony from the school and parents, and decides how the situation should fit the law. This Web site provides information on what the federal laws say and summaries of the rulings interpreting those regulations.

Instant Access Treasure Chest

http://128.172.170.24/ld/ld.html

Helpful information for teacher strategies for teaching all children in the inclusive classroom.

Institute on Community Integration (ICI)

http://ici.umn.edu/

The goal of ICI is to work with the community to improve community services and social support for persons with disabilities and their families.

Research Navigator Guide: Education

Institute on Community Integration: Other Disability-Related Internet Sites

http://ici.umn.edu/relatedresources/
otherwebsites.html

ICI has presented a hyperlinked list of other Internet sites with disability related information

Kids Together, Inc.: Inclusion for Children and Adults with Disabilities

http://www.kidstogether.org/inc.htm

Inclusion for children and Adults with disabilities provides resources for parents, and educators. This site is designed to provide helpful information and resources to enhance the quality of life for children and adults with disabilities, and communities as a whole.

Positive Behavioral Support

http://www.beachcenter.org/frames.php3?id=56

Many feel that positive behavioral support is a critical element in the success of supported inclusion in the schools.

Special Education Resources for K–12

http://falcon.jmu.edu/~ramseyil/specialed.htm

This site will provide information on topics of exceptionality using AskEric InfoGuides, and Professional Organizations. It also provides informational links to Special Education in general, as well as to Attention Deficit Disorder, Autism, Blind & Visually Impaired, Deaf & Hearing Impaired, Learning Disabilities, and Psychiatric Disorders.

Yoga for the Special Child

http://www.specialyoga.com./

Yoga for the Special Child is an integrated system of yoga techniques designed to stimulate the cognitive and motor development of children with Down Syndrome, Cerebral Palsy, Attention Deficit Disorder and Learning Disabilities.

Research Navigator Guide: Education

GIFTED/TALENTED

The Center for Talent Development Network

`http://www.ctd.northwestern.edu/`

The Center for Talent Development Network provides a wealth of materials, activities, and programs for gifted students. This site contains information on the Midwest Talent search, LetterLinks and EPGY, and Saturday Enrichment. These programs provide coursework via distance learning and online. Presented are numerous opportunities for the disciplined gifted student. Fishnet is a special page which permits the student to search for colleges and universities.

Future Problem Solving Program

`http://www.fpsp.org`

The Future Problem Solving Program is available in all fifty states and in a number of foreign countries. The program is constructed on the basis of a six step problem solving process. This process is similar to a number of other creative thinking or critical thinking skills program. The six steps are: identify 20 problems in a number of category areas; identify the underlying problem; identify 20 possible solutions to the underlying problem using a number of categories; generate criteria to judge the ten best solutions; evaluate the ten best solutions; and develop an action plan. The program is available at the primary level, the early adolescent level, and the adolescent to young adult level. This page contains numerous resources for students and teachers.

G/T: Home Page

`http://www.millville.cache.k12.ut.us/tag/gifted2.htm`

This site provides a publications list, schools and programs, articles for parents and teachers, and "funstuff." The "funstuff" section is an annotated list of higher level thinking activities for gifted students. This section is well worth a visit.

Gifted Child Society, Inc.

`http://www.gifted.org/`

This page has a nice simple layout, and the contents will be of benefit to parents, students, and teachers. The site was designed by the parents of gifted students in New Jersey, and contains content written by parents, teachers, and students. The site provides a model for other parent organizations or for students who are interested in web page construction.

Gifted Resources: Talent Searches

`http://www.eskimo.com/~user/ztsearch.html`

This page provides a listing on numerous regional and national enrichment programs for G/T students. Most of the organizations are hyperlinked to provide for ease of viewing the many programs offered.

Helping Your Highly Gifted Child

`http://www.kidsource.com/kidsource/content/`
`help.gift.html`

This page has been sponsored by the US Department of Education. The page is a hypertext version of ERIC EC Digest, number E477. The page discusses the differences of highly gifted children, the needs of these children, and the educational experiences of these children.

National Association for Gifted Children

`http://www.NAGC.org/`

NAGC is one of the most important organizations for the gifted community and is the parent organization for the state organizations. The "frames" compress the appearance of the page. The page provides much information (the use of photoshop would enhance the appearance of this page). NAGC provides annual conferences and is a source of sound literature for parents and teachers.

Gifted Education

`http://www.austega.com/gifted/`

On this site information is provided on how to teach gifted children.

National Research Center on the Gifted and Talented

`http://curry.edschool.virginia.edu/gifted/NRC/`

The University of Virginia maintains this site. Information on research projects conducted by the center can be found here.

The Roeper Review

`http://www.roeperreview.org/`

The Roeper Review has long been recognized as offering current and rigorous research on gifted education. This site is the official site of this journal.

Research Navigator Guide: Education

Talented and Gifted Bibliography

http://www.swopnet.com/ed/TAG/TAG_Bibliography.html

This site provides a few hyperlinks and an extensive bibliography on gifted education.

Gender Equity

Working Definition of Gender Equity in Education

http://www.edc.org/WomensEquity/about/define.htm

This Web site offers a working definition of gender equity in education.

Ideas for Integrating Women of NASA into your Curriculum

http://quest.arc.nasa.gov/women/teachingtips.html

This page suggests ideas to integrate the Women of NASA interactive project into teaching and learning.

All One Heart, "Promoting Diversity Tolerance Through Education"

http://www.alloneheart.com

Discusses issues regarding tolerance of all races and genders.

GENDER EQUITY: FEMALES

Advancing Women: Women's Role in Education

http://www.advancingwomen.com/womedu.html

This article discusses the facts that the teaching profession is predominately female and that the beginning salaries are lower than those for any other field requiring a bachelors degree. It goes on to propose that the few men in the school system dominate and exercise the control.

American Association of University Women

http://www.aauw.org/

This national organization has as it mission to promote education and equity for all women and girls. Their Web site is a source of current research on gender equity, such as the gender gap which exists in our schools, single-sex education for females, sexual harassment in the school hallways. It also contains information on implications for educators, for parents and for the females themselves.

Research Navigator Guide: Education

Feminist Majority Foundation

`http://www.feminist.org/`

A mega-site which connects not only to major feminist organizations, but also connects to informational sites on issues important to many women, such as breast cancer, equity in career opportunity, affirmative action, reproductive rights, feminist arts, literature and entertainment.

Gender Equity in Education

`http://www.nowldef.org/html/issues/edu/links.htm`

The National Organization for Women: Legal Defense and Education Fund (LDEF) seeks to define and defend women's rights. The NOW Web site provides access to information about specific issues of interest to the organization, of which gender equity in education is one.

Gender Equity in Education: Additional Resources

`http://www.ed.gov/offices/ODS/g-equity.html`

Multiple links to organizations and resources supporting equity in education for females and other underrepresented groups.

Gender Equity in Sports

`http://bailiwick.lib.uiowa.edu/ge/`

Gender Equity in Sports is a Web site designed to serve as a resource to assist in the investigation of gender equity issues in interscholastic or intercollegiate sports.

The Girl Child

`http://www.unicef.org/voy/meeting/gir/girhome.html`

This site focuses on providing information about discrimination against girls at all ages of development.

InGear: Integrating Gender Equity and Reform

`http://www.ceismc.gatech.edu/ceismc/programs/ingear/homepg.htm`

Despite significant progress over the past decade, the low level of participation by women in areas of science, engineering and mathematics continues to be a national concern. Between now and the year 2000, nearly two-thirds of all new entrants in the work force will be women-but current

Research Navigator Guide: Education

trends indicate that disproportionately few of these women will pursue advanced degrees or professional careers in science, math or engineering.

Martha's Gender Equity Site

```
http://www.crpc.rice.edu/CRPC/GT/mborrow/
GenderEquity/geeqlist.html
```

This site, created by an educator, includes access to gender equity information for educators, parents and females of all ages. Many of the sites focus on women involvement in technology at all levels.

Equity, Diversity and Education Library

```
http://www.colorado.edu/education/BUENO/
bueno_library.html
```

This site discusses the education of diversity and special student populations as well as promoting education equity for all students.

American Association of Affirmative Action

```
http://www.affirmativeaction.org/
```

The American Association for Affirmative Action is a professional association for affirmative action, equal opportunity, diversity and human resources professionals and is dedicated to the elimination of discrimination on the basis of race, gender.

Women in Science

```
http://www.geocities.com/Wellesley/4340/
```

This site shows how women can be involved in Science as well as men can.

Archives for Research on Women and Gender

```
http://www.lib.utsa.edu/Archives/arwg.html
```

A Project of the Center for the Study of Women and Gender.

Women Leaders Online and Women Organizing for Change

```
http://www.wlo.org/home.htm
```

The organization's goal is to build a network of one million women and men to empower women in politics, society, the economy, the media, and cyberspace. They feel that if they have a million members, women will finally have some clout! The Web site provides connections to various sources of information about women's rights.

Women of Color Resource Center

`http://www.coloredgirls.org/`

The Women of Color Resource Center (WCRC), with the aim of developing a firm, institutional foundation for social change activism by and on behalf of women of color, presents links to sites of interest on topics of social change related to economic inequity, racial discrimination, and sexism.

Women Watch: The UN Internet Gateway on the Advancement and Empowerment of Women

`http://www.un.org/womenwatch/index.html`

Access to "The UN Working for Women", "UN Global Conferences and Women", "Women of the World" which includes regional plans of action for women's advancement and empowerment; statistical information and various other Internet resources on women. Connections to other sources of international and national interest available, including on-line conferences and listservs.

Women's Studies

`http://home.earthlink.net/~dboals1/nativam.html`

Many links to multiple sites for social studies teachers and others on Women's Issues.

GENDER EQUITY: MALES

Sexual Abuse of Males

`http://www.jimhopper.com/male-ab/`

Resources, info, and support for male survivors of incest and sexual abuse.

Men's Issues in Academia

`http://www.vix.com/men/school/school.html`

Issues relating to males in education, such as the gender gap in education, i.e., the underrepresentation of males pursuing education as a career and other related issues.

Men's Issues Links

http://www.geocities.com/capitalHill/6708/
menlinks.html

An electronic link to Web sites on men's issues, such as: dispelling gender myths, inequities in the judicial against men, etc. Also provides links to men's magazines and organizations.

National Organization for Men against Sexism Web Site

http://www.nomas.org/

The National Organization for Men Against Sexism (NOMAS) is an activist organization of men and women supporting positive changes for men. NOMAS advocates a pro-feminist, gay affirmative, anti-racist perspective which is committed to justice on a broad range of social issues including class, age, religion, and physical abilities. The organization maintains that the ultimate expression of what it means to be "male" is to endeavor to make this nation's ideals of equality substantive.

Online Commentaries on Men in Teaching:

http://www.vix.com/men/school/maleteacher.html
http://www.vix.com/men/school/whynomaleteach.html

World Wide Web Virtual Library: The Men's Issues Page

http://www.vix.com/men/

The goal of this site is to provide a collection of electronic resources which provide links to information related to the men's movement, such as comprehensive reference lists of men's movement organizations, books, periodicals, web links and other related resources. In addition, this site seeks to serve as an online reference source for statistics, studies and bibliographies of interest to the men's movements.

FATHERING, INCLUDING DIVORCE AND CUSTODY-RELATED ISSUES

American Coalition for Father's and Children (ACFC): Father's Rights for Gender Equity

http://www.acfc.org/

ACFC is dedicated to the creation of a family law system, legislative system, and public awareness which promotes equal rights for ALL parties affected by divorce, and the breakup of a family or establishment of paternity. Links to support shared parenting and joint custody are provided.

Research Navigator Guide: Education

National Center for Fathering

http://www.fathers.com

Organization supporting the involvement of fathers in the lives of their children. Links to legal topics and practical topics, as well as other father-friendly sites.

Choice for Men

http://www.nas.com/c4m/

"Choice for Men" is a cause supporting the idea that a man has the right to make the decision whether or not to terminate his parental rights and responsibilities (not a court, as in adoption). It gives men a right that women have had since 1973 and Roe v. Wade . . . to decline parenthood. It also permits men to plan their families free from government intrusion.

Father's Rights Foundation

http://www.fathers-rights.com/index.html

A Web page dedicated to the fight For Fathers Rights, with links to legal and informational sites.

The Father's Role in Society

http://www.vix.com/pub/men/nofather/articles/amneus.html

There is a widespread concern about crime, educational failure, drugs, social decay, etc. and the perception that these are connected with family breakdown, in particular with the erosion of the weakest link in the family, the father's role. This Web page provide opportunities to study and discuss these topics.

Fatherhood & Fatherlessness

http://www.vix.com/pub/men/nofather/nodad.html#dad

Many articles are stated in which deal with these topics. One article describes why children need their father. It also gives detail of fatherlessness.

For Fathers, Separated, Divorced, Non-custodial

http://www.divorcedfather.com/

The purpose of the Web site is to validate the feelings felt by fathers not living with their children and to affirm the conviction that a father can still say involved in their children's lives, even though not present in the children's home. Weblinks to other sites providing information and support on joint parenting are available.

National Fatherhood Initiative (NFI)

http://www.fatherhood.org/

The mission of NFI is to improve the well-being of children by increasing the number of children growing up with loving, committed and responsible fathers involved in their children's lives.

Fathers and Families

http://www.fathersandfamilies.org/

A Massachusetts based non-profit organization advocating for the right of every child to have two parents regardless of divorce or separation.

MARITAL STATUS

NJ Statewide Nontraditional Career Assistance Center

http://www.equitynj.org/

This site covers gender equity, diversity and single parent issues. This site also offers research, news and events concerning gender equity.

Family: Single Parenting

http://www.parentsplace.com/family/archive/
0,10693,239458,00.html

General resources on single parenting, many on single mothers, and far less on single fathers.

Second Wives Crusade

http://www.secondwives.org/

This organization believes that all children deserve equal rights and protection under the law and supports equity and fairness for all families.

RESOURCES FOR SUPPORTING AND MODELING GENDER EQUITY IN THE CLASSROOM

Action Guide for Girl's Education

http://www.igc.org/beijing/ngo/girls.html

Research Navigator Guide: Education

This is a network of volunteer groups of teachers, parents, writers, sociologists, and academicians dedicated to raising awareness of educational access and equity for girls around the world. There is a commitment to closing the gender gap—the predominance of boys over girls.

Beyond Pink and Blue

`http://osu.orst.edu/~huj/512/intro.html`

This Web site discusses the traditional male and female colors and toys. They give examples of advertisements and marketing techniques that show how certain colors and toys are assigned to boys or girls.

Colors, Toys, and the Invisible Sexism

`http://osu.orst.edu/~huj/512/ccc.html`

Pictures that propose that the use of bright primary colors traditionally used in preschool setting is biased towards boys. This Web site advocates the integration of light pastel colors in the classroom.

Design Your Future: Math, Science and Technology for Girls

`http://www.autodesk.com/dyf/dyfmain2.html`

Generally, girls interests wanes in 5th or 6th grade for science and math, lower opportunities for them to pursue careers in the underrepresented areas. "Design Your Future: Math, Science, and Technology for Girls" is an educational initiative to support and encourage girls in pursuing careers in Math, Science and technology.

Expect the Best from a Girl—That's What You'll Get

`http://www.academic.org/`

This site supports a national campaign for educational equity for girls in their early teens; includes links to programs, career resources advice for parents and educators, etc.

Familyeducation.com

`http://www.familyeducation.com/`

This is a search engine that accesses information on parenting issues in raising open minded, empathetic children and teaching them an understanding of differences among people. This site also involves current topics to choose from; preschool & younger, Elementary school, Middle school, High school, and beyond.

Parent Library "Boys Will Be Boys" and Other Myths by Lilian G. Katz

http://npin.org/library/pre1998/n00190/n00190.html

Topics include; Biology or Society, Aggression & Play, and Peer Pressure and their effects on boys.

A Parent's Dilemma, A Transgender Child

http://indigo.ie/~transgen/dilemma.htm

Support for parents who may have a transgender child.

Reexamining the Plight of Young Males

http://www.washingtonpost.com/wp-srv/national/longterm/gender/gender26a.htm

Discussion of support for males who like colors, toys, activities that are generally thought of to be "girls" colors, toys and activities.

Girlstart Home Page

http://www.girlstart.org/

The mission of this resource is to encourage girls (particularly middle school) in math, science, engineering and technology through hands-on activities and role models. The organization attempts to provide strategies and resources to encourage young women to pursue their education and careers in science, math and engineering.

Snips, Snails, and Puppy Dog Tails, Girls and Boys

http://babyparenting.about.com/library/weekly/aa030698.htm?terms=snips+snails+girls+boys

This site gives information about various differences between girls and boys. It also gives advice on parenting babies and toddlers, both male and female.

Wellness 10: Gender Equity

http://www.sasked.gov.sk.ca/docs/wellness/gender.html

Teacher tips are provided for accomplishing gender equity in the classroom.

Women's History Month

http://socialstudies.com/c/Pages/womenindex.html

This is a Web site where lesson plans, web exercises are available for Women's Month. Also present are reviews of curriculum materials and its level of support for gender equity.

Writing With Gender-Fair Language

```
http://www.rpi.edu/dept/llc/writecenter/web/
genderfair.html
```

Examples of how to implement gender-fair language are provided here. This could be useful to both teachers and parents.

Language

The American Language and Culture Institute

```
http://www.csusm.edu/alci/
```

California State at San Marcos maintains this page to offer educators a variety of English as a Second Language experiences.

Bilingual Education

```
http://psrtec/clmer.csulb.edu/bilingedu.html
```

An excellent resource page on bilingual education. All of the resources are hyperlinked for ease of review. In addition, brief annotations appear with each reference. Some of the references are as follows: Office of Bilingual Education and Minority Languages Affairs, National Clearinghouse for Bilingual Education, Linguistic Minorities Research Institute, and National Association for Bilingual Education.

Children and Bilingualism

```
http://www.kidsource.com/asha/bilingual.html
```

About 32 million people in the U.S. speak a language other than English in their homes. This page offers some resources and links to resources for helping these children in the schools.

Clip Art Collection for Foreign/Second Language Instruction.

```
http://www.sla.purdue.edu/fll/JapanProj/FLClipart/
```

This site offers a nice collection of royalty-free clip art for bilingual education.

Cross-Cultural and Cross-Lingual Links

```
http://pegasus.cc.ucf.edu/~abrice/Cross-cultural.html
```

Research Navigator Guide: Education

This well maintained site by Alexjandro Brice is an excellent research site. The site contains the following resources: conferences, connections (email exchanges), resources, professional associations, professional journals, and hypertext of research.

Yamada Language Guides

http://babel.uoregon.edu/yamada/guides.html

The Yamada WWW Language Guides are the definitive guide to language resources on the World Wide Web.

Dave's ESL Cafe

http://www.eslcafe.com

Dave Perling has an international reputation for working with TESOL and ESL. This page is well designed. The page is a long scrolling page with the 26 characters of the alphabet as a table of contents. The page provides a chat central, discussion center, graffiti wall, hints, help center, and many other educator resources.

Ebonics: Look Who's Talking

http://www.afronet.com/WB/040497-3.html

This page is an essay on the incorporation of ebonics into the curriculum.

For Teachers

http://www.unhcr.ch/teach/teach.htm

The United Nations sponsors this official site for teacher resources for teaching refugees. The page is linked to many other UN resources. A special bibliography is provided that list numerous annotated teaching resources.

Impact! Online

http://lrs.ed.uiuc.edu/Impact/impact_homepage.html

The Department of Educational Psychology at University of Illinois assists in maintaining this site. The site is an interactive news magazine for intermediate and advanced ESL/EFL students. Highlighted words are hyperlinked to explanations and to audio files for pronunciation assistance.

The Language Project

http://www.langproj.demon.co.uk/

Research Navigator Guide: Education

The purpose of the Language project is to provide teacher education courses in teaching English as a second language. The page provide a good deal of specific information about the process used. There is even a hyperlink to au pairs.

The National Clearinghouse for Bilingual Education (NCBE)

`http://www.ncbe.gwu.edu`

This clearinghouse is funded by OBEMLA to collect, analyze, and disseminate information relating to the effective education of linguistically and culturally diverse learners in the U.S. help bilingual learners.

Native Languages Page

`http://www.nativeculture.com/lisamitten/natlang.html`

This is a well maintained page on native languages. The page has been hyperlinked to many resources. Some of the languages which are referenced are Arapaho, Cherokee, Cheyenne, Chippewa, Dakota, and Navajo.

Office of Bilingual Education and Minority Languages Affairs

`http://www.ed.gov/offices/OBEMLA/`

This is the official home page which explains the Bilingual Education Act in 1968 in recognition of the growing number of linguistically and culturally diverse children enrolled in schools.

Terralingua

`http://www.terralingua.org/`

Terralingua has two main goals: preserving the world's linguistic diversity, and investigating connections between biological and cultural diversity. This university maintained page provides several resources for preserving linguistic diversity. The resource list at **http://cougar.ucdavis.edu/nas/ terralin/endlangs.html** provides an annotated listing of organizations working on linguistic diversity issues. An important feature is that many of these organizations are now hyperlinked.

Welcome to ESL Net!

`http://esl.net/`

This site lists a number of U.S. and International ESL schools. The site provides a resource section which is hyperlinked to several ESL references.

Ideas for working with ESL students

http://education.indiana.edu/cas/tt/v2i2/ideas.html

Teacher Talk is a resource for pre-service teachers, especially at the secondary level, and provides practical ideas for pre-service students and those who are students teaching.

Bilingual Families Web Page

http://www.nethelp.no/cindy/biling-fam.html

Bilingual parents can find information and resources here to help them raise their children bilingually. This site talks about the myths and politics of Bilingualism among other things.

Provision of English-as-a-Second-Language Instruction by Speech-Language Pathologists in School Settings

http://professional.asha.org/multicultural/esl_slp.cfm

Race/Ethnicity

AFRICAN AMERICAN

African-American Issues

http://www.black-collegian.com/african/index.shtml

This is a must site for the study of multiculturalism. The site contains numerous articles of current interest and numerous articles of historical interest.

African-American Population Statistics

http://www.lenzine.com/census/index.htm

A U.S. Department of Commerce site. This page contains numerous tables and charts which are African-American centered. Topics include general population, education, marital status, economics, employment and poverty. This site contains a wealth of data for the study of African-American issues.

Comer School Development Program

http://info.med.yale.edu/comer/

James B. Comer, M.D. of Yale University has developed a very promising plan for the implementation of multiculturalism in the public schools. The School Development Program home page provides an outstanding model for educational improvements. The guiding principle of the SDP are no-fault, consensus, and collaboration. Student achievement at Comer schools has risen significantly.

Gravity

http://newsavanna.com/gravity/

This is an excellent multicultural page. This page is the successor page to the Meanderings Home Page.

The Faces of Science: African Americans in the Sciences

http://www.princeton.edu/~mcbrown/display/faces.html

This Web page lists African American men and women who have contributed to the advancement of science and engineering. African American chemists, biologists, inventors, engineers, and mathematicians have contributed in both large and small ways that can be overlooked when chronicling the history of science. This site may offer great encouragement to future generations.

Meanderings Home Page

http://newsavanna.com/meanderings

This is an electronic journal which offers some articles on sensitive political issues. The primary articles are concerned with issues of interest to African American and to readers of African American literature. The site may be controversial. Teachers will find a wealth of materials, but may want to monitor or select given issues for student research. This site offers various viewpoint about diversity issues. The past journals are not always the most recent writings on issues.

Race and Ethnicity

http://www.webactive.com/directory/wniadirsearch.html
?Race+and+Ethnicity

This site contains numerous links to other Web sites. This is a comprehensive ethnicity site. The home page for this site lists many resources for the student.

ASIAN AMERICANS

Asian Arts

http://www.webart.com/asianart/index.html

This is a serious site which offers numerous examples of Asian artwork. Often artwork is accompanied by full commentary.

Asia Society

http://www.asiasociety.org

This is a premier site. The Asia Society is America's leading institution dedicated to fostering an understanding of Asia and communication between Americans and the peoples of Asia and the Pacific. The Asia Society presents a wide range of programs including major art exhibitions, performances, international corporate conferences, and contemporary affairs programs.

Asian Studies WWW Virtual Library

http://coombs.anu.edu.au/WWWVL-AsianStudies.html

This site provides the following data: online resources for Asian studies, conferences, databases and Asia-Pacific mailing lists, academic programs and resources for studying abroad in Asia, regional, country and subject-oriented mailing lists, online Asian Studies' journals and newsletters, online Bookshops, searchable catalogs of Asian Studies' bookshops and publishers.

China News Digest

http://www.cnd.org

This site is maintained by the Asian American Network. The site provides information about current events in China, short stories and photos of China. There is some Chinese language on this site.

National Asian American Telecommunication Society

http://www.naatanet.org

NAATA is one site created to provide culturally diverse programming for public television. NAATA's program areas have expanded to include support to media artists, international educational, and cable distribution.

National Clearinghouse for U.S.-Japan Studies

http://www.indiana.edu/~japan

This site is maintained by Indiana University. The site is very creative and current. A visit to Virtual Japan provides video, maps, readings, news, and travel information.

Stanford Guide to Japan Information Resources

http://bases.stanford.edu/USATMC/jguide

Another university page, this site provides information on current topics in Japan. Some Japanese language is available.

HISPANIC AMERICANS

Hispanic Page in the U.S.

http://coloquio.com/index.html

This site has won a number of awards. The site is enhanced by a number of interesting graphics which load very fast. The site lists several famous historic Hispanics. Also listed are connections to all Latin American nations. Current developments in Spain are cited. A very good set of links are provided.

Hispanic Culture Center

http://hcfoundation.org/

A bilingual Web site claiming to be the "largest and most comprehensive facility of its kind in the United States." The center is programmatically linked to schools communities and cultural institutions around the world.

LatinoWeb

http://latinoweb.com/

This Web site is a virtual info center for businesses and nonprofit organizations.

U.S. Census Bureau Hispanic Population

http://www.census.gov/population/www/socdemo/hispanic.html

This site provides census data on the U.S. Hispanic population. Current population survey are summarized in data tables. Official definitions of the term *Hispanic* are provided.

Welcome to Amigos

http://edweb.sdsu.edu/people/cguanipa/amigos/

A professional site that will benefit Hispanics and others interested in studying Hispanics. The site provides informational essays, resources for locating help, stories of intergenerational experiences. This is a very user friendly and highly interactive page.

NATIVE AMERICAN

Index of Native American Resources on the Internet

http://www.hanksville.org/NAresources/

This is a very well maintained site. A table specifies over thirty subjects dealing with Native culture such as education, culture, books, music, and video. There are approximately 700 different referring pages that send accesses to this Index. Approximately 170 of these referring pages are from search engines, leaving about 500 other referring pages that sent one or more accesses to this Index. The Index is accessed about 350 times a day.

A Line in the Sand

http://www.hanksville.org/sand/

This is a Native American site; this site deals with issues of cultural property which includes not only land and other tangible property, but also ideas, traditions, and other non-tangibles. The site explores cultural stereotypes, ethics in archaeology and anthropology, and cultural suppression. Both fiction and nonfiction references are provided. This site is being developed into a commercial CD-ROM permitting students to study these issues without being online.

The Institute of Tribal Environmental Professionals

http://www4.nau.edu/itep

The Institute of Tribal Environmental Professionals was established in support of environmental protection of Native American natural resources. The institute provides training and educational programs for Indian tribes.

Native American

http://home.earthlink.net/~dboals1/nativam.html

This site by Dennis Boals currently lists 139 links to Native American resources. The Boals site is a true mega-site for a variety of research interests. This site is well suited for public school and higher education research. The information provided is unbiased, and does provide for a comprehensive review of many electronic data sites.

Native American Home Pages

http://www.nativeculture.com/lisamitten/indians.html

Lisa Mitten at the University of Pittsburgh maintains this current collection of resources. The web mistress is a mixed-blood Mohawk urban Indian, and a librarian at the University of Pittsburgh. The goal is to provide access to home pages of individual Native Americans and Nations, and to other sites that provide solid information about American Indians. This page is organized by the following categories: Information on Individual Native Nations, Native Organizations and Urban Indian Centers, Tribal Colleges, Native Studies Programs, Native Media-Organizations, Journals and Newspapers, Radio and Television, Powwows and Festivals, Sources for Indian Music, Native Arts Organizations and Individuals, Native Businesses, and links to native American home pages.

Native American News

www.nanews.org/index2.shtml

This site has been updated weekly by Gary Night Owl; the site is about those who walk the Red Road. This site provides a Native American newsletter online and also posts back issues.

NativeNet

http://niikaan.fdl.cc.mn.us/natnet/

This page has been designed as a research link to indigenous people from all nations. The page maintains electronic mailing lists, archives, references, and history concerning indigenous people of the world. This page provides online newsletters from the American Indian Library Association.

Native Web

www.nativeweb.org

The site "touches ancient teaching and modern technology." The categories of this site include the following: Subject Categories, Geographic Regions, Nations/Peoples, Languages, Education, Law & Legal Issues, Literature, Women, Newsletters & Journals, Organizations, Bibliographies, Historical Material, K–12 Sites, Information Sites, Dictionaries, Personal Home Pages, and Mailing lists.

OTHER ETHNIC PAGES

All Things Irish

http://www.Ireland.com

This site is searchable by keyword. This is a very comprehensive Irish page. The page is maintained by an American to provide information about Ireland for interested users.

America's Stirfry: Home Page

www.americas-stirfry.com

This is a commercial site whose primary focus is to cultivate a positive self-esteem and self-image in children of all colors. People of color have made great contributions to the United States. The site offers resources to educators.

Centerville Sister Cities

http://www.ci.centerville.oh.us/sistercity/

This is a page that the authors of this text have designed. The page is hosted on the City of Centerville, OH server. This informational site permits residents to communicate with European and Canadian sister cities. The page provides a historical overview, current projects and several links. This page is included to demonstrate how local citizens might think "globally."

Diversity Resources

http://www.ed.wright.edu/diversity/
ethnicracediversi.htm

This is a comprehensive site for many resources concerning diversity issues. After linking to this site, click on Ethnicity or directly access the address at **http://www.ed.wright.edu/cehs/diversity/ethnic.race. diversi.htm.** This mega-site contains many ethnic links to the following areas: Native American, Asian Americans, African Americans, Hispanic Americans, and other diversity links.

Electronic Ellis Island

http://wwwald.bham.wednet.edu/museum/museum.htm

The mission statement is to chronicle and celebrate the diversity of the many cultures around our world through the eyes of children. The International Channel in cooperation with the Ellis Island Immigration Museum, The Statue of Liberty-Ellis Island Foundation and the National Park Service invite the user to take a tour of Ellis Island.

Ellis Island—Through America's Gateway

http://www.internationalchannel.com/education/ellis

Similar to the Electronic Ellis Island site. This site also has many photographs and some film clips on immigration.

Hajj Travel Web Page

http://www.geocities.com/al_hajj/Travel.html

This site provides an overview of the reasons for this pilgrimage to Mecca. The site reviews all of the necessary preparations required for the pilgrimage.

Iranian Cultural and Information Center

http://tehran.stanford.edu

Notice that the URL is from Stanford. This is a non-controversial site which represents historical and current Iran. The site covers history, art, travel, photos, and other resources.

Judaism and Jewish Resources

http://shamash.org/trb/judaism.html

This is a comprehensive Jewish study page. Contents covers Hebrew, Yiddish, the Holocaust, Israel, museums, art, travel, and many related subjects.

The Human Rights Campaign

http://www.hrc.org/

This site was selected by POINT as one of the Top 5% Best Sites on the Net! The Human Rights Campaign envisions an America where lesbian and gay people are ensured of their basic equal rights, and can be open, honest and safe at home, at work, and in the community.

The Mideast Peace Process

http://www.israel-mfa.gov.il/mfa/go.asp?MFAH000c0

This page is updated to reflect recent events. An effort is made to provide both Israeli and Palestinian perspectives and history.

The National Italian American Foundation

http://www.niaf.org

This site contains information about Italian and Italian-Americans, such as Italian/Italian-American organizations, Famous Italians/Italian-Americans, History, Genealogy, Music, and much more.

National Multicultural Institute

http://www.nmci.org//

The national multicultural Institute is primarily concerned with offering multicultural training. This page offers training information, resources and several important links to other multicultural sites.

The Nordic Page

http://www.markovits.com/nordic/

The following subjects are provided on this page: general information about the Nordic countries, Official home pages, news, Nordic Cities, Arts

& culture, Business and Education. This site provides links of interests to the student of Nordic countries. The clickable map of Norway is very good. Be prepared for Scandinavian languages in navigating this site.

The Study of Russia

http://lcweb2.loc.gov/frd/cs/rutoc.html

This site takes a look in brief at various cultural traits of Russia.

Sister Cities International

http://www.sister-cities.org

This is a true premier site for honest ethnic exchanges. Sister Cities International was conceived by President Eisenhower in the 1950's. This organization has grown greatly during the past one-half century. The annual international conference provides an excellent international forum for an exchange of ideas. Moreover, Sister Cities International offers an opportunity for students to conference and to communicate.

Standards: An International Journal of Multicultural Studies

http://www.colorado.edu/journals/standards/

An electronic journal of multicultural studies.

United Nations

http://www.un.org

This is an official site provided by the UN Information is available in English, Spanish, and French. This site will be of great value to multicultural students. The information is current, and searches are available to the user.

United States Holocaust Museum

http://www.ushmm.org

This museum is a must visit for all Americans. However, a virtual visit to this Web site will provide a strong flavor of the actual museum.

LESSON AND RESOURCE PAGES

American Immigration Home Page

http://www.bergen.org/AAST/Projects/Immigration/

This site contains a good deal of data on past and current immigration. The site is maintained by the Academy for the Advancement of Science and Technology.

Demography and Population Studies WWW VL

http://demography.anu.edu.au/VirtualLibrary/

This site contains over 172 links for democracy and population studies. This international site is maintained by the Australian National University.

Intercultural Email Classroom Connections

http://www.iecc.org/

Intercultural Email Classroom Connections is a free service to help link teachers and classes from different countries and cultures via email for pen-pal and other exchanges. This is a very well maintained site. Both teachers and students will enjoy the benefits of immediately establishing a relationship with a "web-pal."

Institute of International Education

http://www.iie.org

This page provides information on Fullbright Fellowships. In addition, the site offer much information concerning international educational exchanges. A search tool provides assistance in navigating this page.

Legal Information Institute

http://supct.law.cornell.edu/supct/

This site is developed on the basis of the U.S. Supreme Court electronic project, Hermes. Provides current Court decisions from 1990–present. While this is a general site, it is important to the review of specific multicultural Court cases.

Library of Congress

http://www.loc.gov/

This is a mega-site containing a good deal of research data. This site is included in this section because the site also has a number of important multicultural resources. Searchable resources are provided.

National Geographic Online

http://www.nationalgeographic.com

The journal has been an educational tool for over one hundred years. While the full journal is not available at this site, the online version is still an important resource.

Population Reference Bureau

http://www.prb.org/

This is a fantastic research page for studying the population and demography of over 200 nations. A specific search engine for populations statistics and resources are provided. Links to many other sites are available. A specific sub directory on education should be of value to teachers in developing lesson plans. This sub directory also provides many other educational resources about population studies.

Teaching African-American History

http://socialstudies.com/c/Pages/blackhistory.html

This commercial site is maintained by Social Studies school service. The site is an online version of the catalog. In addition, several links are provided for teaching about African American History.

Teaching Diversity

http://fisher.osu.edu/diversity/teach.htm

This site offers some important tips for teachers in working with student diversity.

The Smithsonian

http://www.si.edu

This is a mega-site. While the site contains much information and links which transcend a multicultural direction, this site is an important multicultural resource site. A site search tool will permit the user to focus on multiculturalism and diversity.

U.S. Census Bureau

http://www.census.gov

An excellent research site. The site is a wealth of statistical information. A "Just for Fun" section is designed to peak student interest in using census information in a learning environment.

United States Immigration and Nationality Act, Title 8

http://www4.law.cornell.edu/uscode/8

Immigration is an important aspect of diversity. This site contains legal research. An essential feature of this site is that the entire searchable code is provided. This information will offer tremendous value to the serious researcher.

Flags of the World

http://www.crwflags.com/fotw/flags/

This is a site originally established by an individual. The site has an excellent display of flags of most nations. National databases are also provided.

Global Village

http://www.servinggod.org/Missionaries/
Global_Village.htm

This site asks the question: what would the world be like if it only had a population of 1000 people.

Sexual Orientation

And Justice for All Home Page

http://www.qrd.org/qrd/www/orgs/aja/

The mission statement of this site is to provide for equality for all regardless of sexual orientation. An essential feature of this site is an extensive set of hyperlinks from the following categories: national, international, regional (US), college organizations, media, legal and political, AIDS/HIV, transgender, campaigns and events, and other resources.

Answers to Your Questions about Sexual Orientation and Homosexuality

http://www.apa.org/pubinfo/orient.html

The American Psychological Association maintains this site as an educational site. The following information is discussed: sexual orientation, causes of sexual orientation, homosexuality, parenting, outing, prejudice and discrimination, therapy, education, and references.

Ask Noah about Sexuality

http://www.noah-health.org/english/sexuality/
sexuality.html

New York Online Access to Health (NOAH) is a project that is sponsored by The City University of New York, The Metropolitan New York Library Council, The New York Academy of Medicine, and The New York Public Library. NOAH is a highly respected medical resource. The NOAH home page provides a listing of several other health aspects. This particular page provides scientific discussions of human sexuality.

The Disparate Classification of Gender and Sexual Orientation in American Psychiatry

http://www.priory.com/psych/disparat.htm

Katherine K. Wilson of the Gender Identity Center of Colorado in Denver has posted a scholarly paper on this site. The entire site is devoted to the contents of the research findings of Dr. Wilson.

Gay and Lesbian Educators

http://www.galebc.org/

This British Columbia organization is dedicated to helping gay and lesbian teachers. The page has sections on the mission, workshops, resources and publications. This site maintains a good set of weblinks for both Canada and for selected nations on gay and lesbian issues.

The Gay, Lesbian, and Straight Education Network (GLSEN)

http://www.glsen.org/templates/index.html

GLSEN is a national organization of teachers, parents, students, and concerned citizens working together to end homophobia in schools. GLSEN strives to assure that each member of every school community is valued and respected, regardless of sexual orientation.

Gender Theory/Gay and Lesbian Culture Studies

http://users.visi.net/~longt/gender.htm

Dr. Thomas Long at the Indiana University of Pennsylvania in dissertation research designed this site for further study. Numerous links are provided in the following areas: sexuality directories, net search engines, academic research, archives and libraries, and vintage book dealers.

Bridges Across the Divide

http://www.bridges-across.org/

The purpose of the Bridges-Across Web site is to provide models and resources for building respectful relationships across the divide in the homosexuality issue.

Human Rights Campaign

http://www.hrc.org/

This is both an educational and an activist site. The site maintains a data base on members of the U.S. House of Representatives and on the U.S. Senate. Member profiles are provides along with voting records. This site permits an email system to representatives and to senators.

HRC'S Online Action Center

http://hrc.policy.net

This page helps identify elected officials.

The Knitting Circle

http://www.sbu.ac.uk/stafflag/resources.html

The South Bank University in the United Kingdom maintains this resource center. Links are provided to numerous scientific resources. The educational resources vary form the Radclyffe Hall Well of Literature to the Bacon Science Laboratory.

National Gay and Lesbian Task Force Youth Institute

http://www.youth.org/loco/ngltfyi/

This site provides a number of resources for gay and lesbian students. Most of the resources are organizations. Phone numbers are listed. Hyperlinks are not provided.

!OutProud!: The National Coalition for Gay, Lesbian, Bisexual & Transgender Youth

http://www.outproud.org/

Provides links to a broad range of resources available for youth and educators on issues supporting Gay, Lesbian, Bisexual & Transgender Youth.

!OutProud!: Resources to be used in School

http://www.outproud.org/school.html

In spite of the fact that the American educational system is founded on the principle of equal access for everyone, many students who are gay, lesbian, bisexual or transgendered are not being accorded equal treatment. Many activists are working hard to make schools a more welcoming place for students, and faculty, of all sexual orientations. This World Wide Web site is designed to interested people organize and advocate regarding this effort.

The P.E.R.S.O.N. Project

http://www.youth.org/loco/PERSONProject/

Public Education Regarding Sexual Orientation Nationally is the name of the organization maintaining this page. An online handbook provides some very good sexuality education resources. Numerous hyperlinks are provided in the following areas: legal resources, hotlines, webpals, organizing tactics, resources, research studies, curricular resources, and an extensive bibliography.

Queer Information

http://www2.cs.cmu.edu/afs/cs/user/scotts/
ftp/bulgarians/mainpage.html

Articles gathered in one place on: coming out, domestic partnership, historic views, nature/nurture basis, religion, political/legal information, etc., provided by the gay, lesbian, bisexual and transgender community.

Rainbow Educators' Network

http://www2.gol.com/users/aidsed/rainbow/

This is a new site for educators concerning sexual orientation. The site is maintained on a regular basis. A site map includes the following: classroom ideas, readings, links, teaching materials, notices and events, and an online survey.

Self-Help & Psychology Magazine: Defining Sexual Orientation

http://www.shpm.com/resources/index.php3/
subcategories.eml

The Self-Help & Psychology Magazine maintains a number of subcategories. The URL listed provides a set of links for several categories. This is a commercial site, and some of the information tends to represent the popular rather than the scientific literature. While fifteen sets of categories are provided, the reader may want to focus on the links titled "gay/lesbian/bisexual/transgendered."

Sexual Orientation: Science, Education, and Policy

http://psychology.ucdavis.edu/rainbow/index.html

This university maintained site provides facts about the following: gays and lesbian sexual orientation, homophobia and how it can be eliminated, stigma of AIDS as a gay disease, stop anti-gay hate crimes, gays in the military. This is a frequently updated site. The links on this page are categorized as science and professional, polls and surveys, hate crimes, HIV/AIDS, policy and legal, education, religious right, other resources, and highly specific.

Sexual Orientation Specific Resources: University of Maryland Diversity Database

http://www.inform.umd.edu/EdRes/Topic/Diversity/
Specific/Sexual_Orientation/index.html

The University of Maryland maintains several diversity pages. This page on sexual orientation provides several resources: announcements, bibliographies, conferences, electronic forums, film reviews, academic papers, and course syllabi.

Talking About Homosexuality in the Secondary School

`http://www.avert.org/talking.htm`

The organization of the site provides information for educators to discuss the following: talking with youth, a discussion of issues concerning gays and lesbians, coming out, discussions with educators, what is homosexuality, homophobia, HIV, and AIDS. This is a very good resource page.

Teen Sexuality

`http://www.intac.com/~jdeck/habib/about.html`

The work of photojournalist Dan Habit is the source of this Web site. This site is a study of several diversity issues. This site may be viewed as a scholarly reference site for those students investigating sexual orientation. The resource page cites actual resources which are important references. None of these resources are hyperlinked, but phone numbers are listed for additional information.

Welcome to Ethics Updates

`http://ethics.acusd.edu/Applied/SexualOrientation`

This site is frequently updated. The material is presented for research information. Summaries of recent literature is provided, and a set of web resources is also provided.

MULTICULTURAL CHILDREN'S LITERATURE: SEXUAL ORIENTATION

Annotated Bibliography of Children's Books with Gay and Lesbian Characters

`http://www.glsen.org/templates/resources/`
`record.html?section=16&record=101`

Resources for early childhood educators and parents.

Sexual Orientation: Science, Education and Policy

`http://psychology.ucdavis.edu/rainbow/index.html`

Dr. Gregory Herek, a noted authority on antigay prejudice (or homophobia), hate crimes, and AIDS stigma, has created this site to provide factual information about sexual orientation and HIV/AIDS. It is the goal of the site to promote the use of scientific knowledge for education and enlightened public policy. Links are available to access legal information, current research and professional literature.

Research Navigator Guide: Education

Other Online Resources

Allyn & Bacon Curriculum and Instruction Supersite

`http://www.ablongman.com/C&I`

This Web site is a wealth of information for pre-service and in-service teachers—whether they want to gain new insights, pick up practical information, or simply connect with one another. Within this Web site you will find:

- Teaching Resources
- Ready-To-Use Lesson Plans and Activities for All Grade-Levels
- Subject-specific Web links for further research and discovery
- Information on Allyn & Bacon professional titles to help you in your teaching career
- Up-To-Date "In The News" features
- ContentSelect for Education
- State Standard Correlations—Content experts correlate the content standards for grades 1–6 and in some cases grades 1–8, for CA, NY, TX, FL, IL, OH specifically to the Allyn & Bacon textbook.

Allyn & Bacon Early Childhood Education Supersite

`http://www.ablongman.com/ECE`

This comprehensive site offers a wealth of information for students preparing for a career in early childhood or for practitioners in an early childhood setting. Featuring a vast collection of lesson plans, teaching resources, weblinks and current events articles written by experts in the field of Early Childhood Education, this site also features:

- ContentSelect for Education
- Up-To-Date "In the News" features
- Instructor's Resources
- Classroom Activities
- Teaching Resources
- Weblinks
- Professional Development Weblinks
- Methods Books
- Professional Books catalog page

Companion Web Sites

`http://www.abinteractive.com/gallery`

Our Companion Web sites use the Internet to provide you with various opportunities for further study and exploration. The CW offers study content and activities related to the text, as well as an interactive, online study guide. Quizzes containing multiple choice, true/false, and essay questions can be graded instantly, and forwarded to your instructor for recording—all online. For a complete list of titles with a CW, visit **www.abinteractive.com/gallery.**